world it cost if

the dog into the

the barbecue

t, where can we

ther lemon stri

IMPORTANT---

Give Claiborne's herbed fried

chicken recipe an extra 10 minutes

a side if you use the electric skillet.

When beef & kidney pie
is done with pie pastry,
ruff pastry, the cooking
~5 mins., not 2 hrs.
recipe on

nksgiving Week

s. eve.
Make soup stock
✓ dishes that seldom
used for cleanliness

eve.
inish (non-cream-based)
soup
Cook 1st-course shrimp
Prepare shrimp sauce
Chop ingredients (but
it combine) bird

Dear---

If the leftovers
of pea soup I've left out
to thaw turn out to be
something else, you can
take me out to dinner.
Otherwise we'll have
pea soup, french bread,
cheese and salad. Love,

N NE

BRAT

c ple

Two in the Kitchen

Drawing by Karla Clement for *The Washington Post*, by permission.

A jug of wine a loaf of bread & Us

Two in the Kitchen

by Joe & Jeanne Anderson

Published by ACROPOLIS BOOKS LTD. • WASHINGTON, D.C. 20009

Acknowledgments

Grateful acknowledgment is made to the publishers listed below for permission to reprint the following:

Excerpt (p. 53) from CRAIG CLAIBORNE'S KITCHEN PRIMER by Craig Claiborne by permission of Alfred A. Knopf, Inc. Copyright (C) 1969 by Craig Claiborne.

Definition of "brunch" (p. 61). By permission. From Webster's New Collegiate Dictionary (C) 1974 by G. & C. Merriam Co., Publishers of the Merriam-Webster Dictionaries.

Recipe for "Salsa Cruda" (p. 68). From the book, ELENA'S SECRETS OF MEXICAN COOKING by Elena Zelayeta. (C) 1958 by Prentice-Hall, Inc. Published by Prentice-Hall, Inc., Englewood Cliffs, New Jersey.

Recipe for "Vichyssoise à la Ritz" (p. 69) from THE NEW YORK TIMES COOK BOOK edited by Craig Claiborne. Copyright (C) 1961 by Craig Claiborne. Reprinted by permission of Harper & Row, Publishers, Inc.

Definitions of "Welsh rabbit" and "omelet" (pp. 123-124). By permission. From Webster's New Collegiate Dictionary (C) 1961 by G. & C. Merriam Co., Publishers of the Merriam-Webster Dictionaries.

Recipe for "Baked Mixed Vegetables" (p. 142) from THE ROUND-THE-WORLD COOK BOOK by Myra Waldo by permission of Doubleday & Co., Inc. Copyright (C) 1954 by Myra Waldo Schwartz.

Recipe for "Crema de Naranja" (Orange Custard, p. 142). From THE SPANISH COOKBOOK by Barbara Norman. Copyright (C) 1969 by Barbara Norman. Published by Bantam Books, Inc. and Atheneum Publishers.

© Copyright 1974 by Joe and Jeanne Anderson

ACROPOLIS BOOKS LTD.
Colortone Building, 2400 17th St., N.W., Washington, D.C. 20009

Printed in the United States of America by
COLORTONE PRESS Creative Graphics, Inc.
Washington, D.C. 20009

Library of Congress Catalog Number 74-5696
International Standard Book Number 87491-388-8 (cloth)

```
Library of Congress Cataloging in Publication Data

Anderson, Joe, 1928-
    Two in the kitchen.

    1. Cookery.  I. Anderson, Jeanne, 1934-    joint
author.  II. Title.
TX715.A5665  1974        641.5        74-5696
ISBN 0-87491-388-8
```

*For the other two,
Judy and Gwyn*

新年快楽

Drawing by Ronalie Clement Peterson for *The Washington Post*, by permission.

Celebrate the Chinese New Year with ethnic dishes such as Szechuan Duck and Chinese Vegetables (see pp. 87-92).

Contents

In the Beginning

What this book is and isn't

THIS IS THE STORY of a four-career family of two (more recently a six-career family of four) that likes to eat. Starting with negligible kitchen skills and, to this day, a negligible-sized kitchen, they built a reputation for surprising, yet classically acceptable, modes of dining. Getting there was most of the fun.

This is not a recipe book, though many of the recipes in it found great critical approval when first published in *The Washington Post*. We extend grateful acknowledgment to *The Post's* food editor, Louise Oettinger, for her help with the original articles, and to The Washington Post Company for permission to reprint material first published by it.

Neither is this book a textbook, though some of the methods described have even won the praise of home economists. (In case you don't know, some home economists have little use for food authors who are not themselves home economists. Fan mail from them was praise indeed.)

This is an adventure story—an adventure best shared by two people who enjoy one another's company, who enjoy eating, who enjoy working with their hands, who don't see as much of one another as they'd like and who, thus, have made the kitchen and dining room as important a part of their home as the living room and bedroom.

You, as two in the kitchen, may be roommates, friends, lovers, siblings, parent and older child, or, like us, man and wife. You may well already be better cooks than we—the family joke is that between the two of us, we total one good cook. But doing it together is something else again. We invite you to try it.

These principles characterize our cooking and are exemplified in the menus and recipes that follow:

—A firm understanding of the limitations of apartment or small-house kitchens and of entertaining without servants;

—Yet a boldness in challenging these limitations with menus that can be largely pre-prepared and later assembled in a few minutes.

—The use of a sound but notably different twist in the preparation of part of each menu;

—Yet a strenuous avoidance of the merely cute.

—The use of one or more ethnic dishes—Chinese, Italian, Mexican or eastern European—to give a touch of unexpected color to the flavors of a basically American, French or British menu.

—The planning of a menu and its preparation in such a manner that, though the two who cook may spend much of the morning in the kitchen, rarely will more than one of them have to leave guests alone for longer than a minute or two at a time.

—Improvising and experimenting together. "Cooking by ear" is learned faster than you may think, and doing it in partnership is less embarrassing than imposing your mistakes on someone else. As you near the end of the book, our recipes will give you more and more opportunity to set your own proportions of ingredients to fit your own tastes.

Throughout the book, we've asked ourselves, "Would we have been able to follow such limited instructions successfully our first year of cooking together?" When the answer was no, we have either given more detailed instructions or eliminated the recipe.

We have *not,* however, tried to dictate just how you divide up the work in the kitchen. In our house the husband usually rolls the pie crust while the wife makes the pie filling. That doesn't mean such a division would work in another kitchen with another set of talents. For some menus later in the book, we do suggest "one of you do (a) while the other does (b)." You decide who does which.

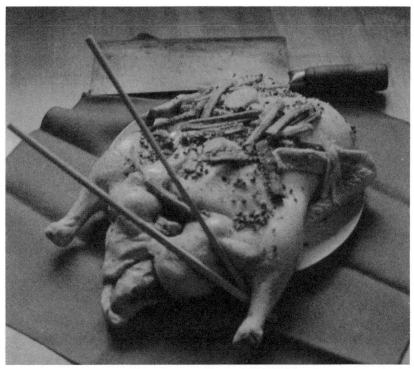

For an unusual menu include one or more ethnic dishes. Here Szechuan Duck is rubbed with Szechuan peppercorns, scallions, and ginger before steaming (see p. 87).

13

For an elegant luncheon or dinner try Lamb Chops with Six Vegetables (see p. 70).

Jumping to the End

**An easy, elegant sample
of the kind of cooking we're discussing**

LET'S TRY THE last chapter first: the easy elegances. Because menu planning is half the job, we'll entertain for six, serving a meat-and-potatoes kind of meal, and make the guests think they've been treated to an even more elegant dinner than, in fact, they have been. With this one menu you can establish many of the pleasures of two in the kitchen; acquiring many of the skills and attitudes can come later.

You start with drinks in the living room. The beef or lamb for which you've paid equivalent pounds of flesh is not for guys who've been guzzling martinis. So you shnocker them into a pre-dinner drink that tastes strong enough and acts weak enough: a tall Negroni.

You plunge onward with a first course of snails, served without the impedimenta which no decent French restaurant could be without, but which no disestablishmentarian home uses without undue pretense. The trick is to stuff the snails in mushrooms.

Serve the roast beef with Yorkshire pudding (or the steak with baked potatoes, the lamb with small oven-roasted potatoes). But surprise the guests with a side dish, a familiar vegetable which is not at all familiar the way you do it: Asparagus East.

You have now served, let us assume, a bottle of white wine (Meursault?) with the snails and two bottles of red (Beauliéu Vineyards Cabernet Sauvignon?) with the meat. (We'll argue another day with the purist who says you don't follow a French wine with an American bottle.) You have been so un-American as to serve the salad *after* the main course, but your guests are so un-continental that not all the red wine is gone. You spring on with a salad, Cognac tomatoes, which does not contain enough acid to kill the remaining wine, which the cheese (Brie, Camembert or Liederkranz) cries for.

Then bring on dessert—apple pie would do, though we suggest crêpes soufflés. The kicker of this course could be a sweet sparkling wine from Italy, a Lacrima Christi or an Aste Spumante. (Again, we'll argue another day with the opponents of sweet wine.)

Every dish on the menu can be prepared largely in advance, with only last-minute fidgeting for the hosts.

Tall Negronis

The Negroni is a cocktail made of equal parts dry gin, sweet vermouth and Bitter Campari. It may be served iced and strained, or on the rocks. It is garnished with an orange slice. But the tall one, which tastes strong but does not kill either the guests or the wine to follow, is thus:

1 pint gin
1 cup Bitter Campari
1 cup sweet vermouth, preferably Punt è Mes
Soda

Mix together ahead of time the gin, Campari and vermouth. As guests arrive, pour for each person 2 or 3 ounces (2 generous shots) of the mixture over ice in an 8- to 10-ounce glass. Finish with soda and

garnish with an orange slice.

Salad à la Russe makes an interesting variation for the salad course (see p. 81).

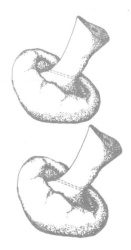

The quart you mixed ahead should serve drinks and refills to six before dinner (not everyone will take a refill), with a little left over for the kitchen cleanup crew the next day.

Snail-Stuffed Mushrooms

1 can of snails (usually 18 snails)

18 large "stuffer" mushrooms

Snail butter (recipe below)

If you own a kitchen scale, follow the can-wrapper recipe for snail butter. If your scale is calibrated in grams as well as ounces, it will be easier to use the proportions in the French or German (grams) recipes than those in English (ounces). Or use the following proportions:

⅔ cup soft butter

1½ teaspoons finely minced shallots

2 large cloves garlic, crushed or minced

1½ tablespoons finely minced parsley

½ teaspoon salt

Several grinds of black pepper

Cream all together. Some add 1½ tablespoons minced celery; others double the parsley. We use 2 tablespoons parsley. This is now snail butter.

Wipe the mushrooms with a damp cloth and, if you wish, brown the tops in an additional 2 tablespoons butter. Remove the stems and save for salad or other uses.

Drain and rinse the snails. Put a half teaspoon of butter in each mushroom, put a snail on top and then top with a half teaspoon or more snail butter. Let stand out for two or three hours in a cake pan. You may sprinkle the snails and mushrooms with a few grinds of nutmeg or some chopped walnuts. Usually we don't bother.

Now comes the only tricky timing of the whole menu. If you have double ovens, you can remove the beef 20 minutes before snails 18 are to be served and raise the heat to 400 degrees (reserving the second oven for Yorkshire pudding). If you have a single oven only, you'll have to take the beef out sooner (no one expects it to be *really* hot anyway) and do the snails during the first 10 minutes the pudding cooks (at 450 degrees).

If at 400 degrees, bake 15 minutes (or 10 minutes in oven and 2 minutes under broiler, if you prefer). If at 450 degrees, bake 10 minutes (the last minute, if you wish, under the broiler). Serve two or three snails per person as an appetizer or first course.

Roast Beef

Buy at least a three-rib standing rib roast, preferably five ribs. (Read the later chapter on planned leftovers.) Wipe roast dry with paper toweling, salt and pepper it on all sides and place in an open roasting pan, bone side down. Place in a 300-degree oven; 20 minutes per pound should bring it to medium rare (145 to 150 degrees on a meat thermometer). No basting.

Yorkshire Pudding

About 10 minutes before taking out the roast (it should rest 20 minutes or more before carving), put 3 or 4 tablespoons of the beef drippings in an 8½-inch square pan. (This makes a puffier pudding than the 11 by 7-inch pan many experts recommend.) Let the pan heat in the oven. As soon as the beef has been removed, raise the oven to 450 degrees.

In a blender, mix together quickly:

2 eggs
1 cup milk
2 cups sifted flour
½ teaspoon salt

Pour into the heated pan and bake 10 minutes; reduce heat to 350 degrees and bake about 15 minutes more or until delicately browned. Cut in squares and serve.

Another method calls for cooking the pudding about 45 minutes at the same temperature as the beef (starting about 25 minutes before

Use leftover roast beef to prepare Beef Mazatlan Style (see p. 102).

the beef is done). This makes a softer center and is, to us, less desirable.

Asparagus East

Call this Chinese asparagus if you wish; we do at home. But most cookbooks use the name Chinese asparagus for 1- to 1½-inch pieces of asparagus which are parboiled, drained, seasoned with MSG and stir-fried. Asparagus East is better. Both asparagus lovers and haters will eat it right up and perhaps not even recognize what vegetable it is.

You'll need eight stalks of asparagus per person, plus butter and soy sauce. Try to get an Oriental soy sauce such as Kikkoman or Amoy, although the flavors of those two are vastly different.

Several hours ahead of time, wash the asparagus well, twirling the flowery tips gently between a thumb and finger under a steady, hard, cold stream of water. With a heavy, sharp Chinese or French knife, cut off the tough stalk at just that point where the knife meets little resistance. (Unless your garbage disposer is still under warranty, put the stalk ends in the can, not the disposer.)

Cut very thin, long diagonal slices. Hold the knife at such an angle that your slices are two or even four times longer than the diameter of the stalk. With a little practice, you will be able to handle several stalks at a time. Leave the flowery tip whole or cut it once lengthwise. Wrap carefully and refrigerate until three minutes before serving.

Heat a 10-inch or larger skillet until it is quite hot. To serve six persons, swirl about 3 tablespoons of butter into the skillet. Drop in the sliced asparagus and fry, stirring continuously, for two minutes and not a second more. Season well with soy sauce (3 tablespoons or to taste) and serve.

Cognac Tomatoes

Put a shallow bed of cleaned watercress or leaf lettuce on each salad plate—2½ bunches of cress should do for six people, leaving   21

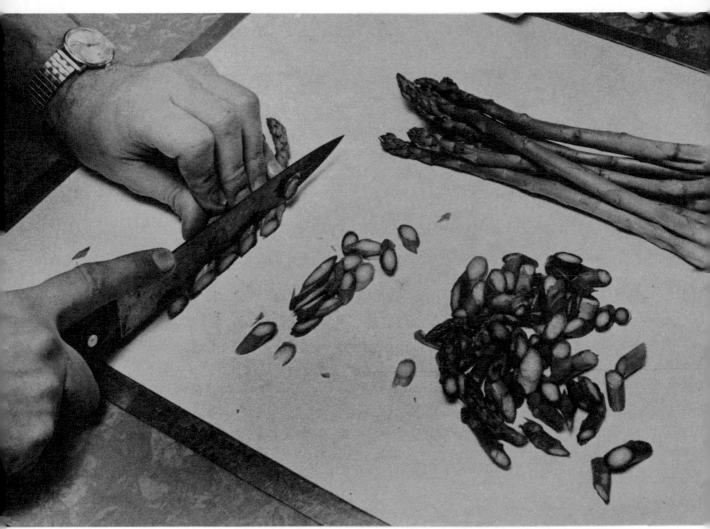

Asparagus East: Cut very thin, long diagonal slices. Hold the knife at such an acute angle that your slices are two or even four times longer than the diameter of the stalk.

half a bunch to garnish the beef. Arrange over each plate one ripe, peeled (see page 82), sliced tomato. Just before serving, sprinkle onto it this dressing:

3 tablespoons oil (olive oil or half-and-half olive and peanut oil)

2 tablespoons good brandy (Cognac or Armagnac)

1 teaspoon salt

⅜ teaspoon freshly ground pepper (or less to taste)

½ teaspoon dried basil, permitted to rest an hour in the pre-mixed dressing, or 2 teaspoons finely chopped fresh basil if you're lucky enough to have it

Accompany the salad with a soft-ripened cheese and with French bread or saltine crackers.

Crêpes Soufflés

If you've not made crêpes before, practice on yourselves once before serving to guests. For your easily elegant dinner, make 12 perfect ones, several hours ahead, to serve six.

¼ pound stick of butter

1 pint milk

2 whole eggs

2 egg yolks

¾ cup flour (unsifted)

2 teaspoons sugar

¼ teaspoon salt

1 teaspoon grated lemon peel

Clarify the butter: melt it gently in a small pan, skim off the foam, then pour the clear fat into another container, discarding the milky solids in the bottom of the pan.

Take 2 tablespoons of the clarified butter, reserving the remainder. Add all the other ingredients and mix well with a whisk, mixer or blender. Let this batter rest for two or three hours—one of you may make the batter while the other fries the breakfast bacon.

To do it the easy way, you will need a 5- or 6-inch skillet or crepe   23 pan plus a well-seasoned 8- to 10-inch skillet. Heat both until quite hot—a drop of water disappears instantly—and brush (using a pastry brush) with the clarified butter. Pour about 2 tablespoons of the batter into the smaller pan, swirl it around to coat the bottom and pour off (back into the bowl!) any excess batter. Cook until a rim of brown appears around the pancake. At this point, the expert will flip the crêpe with a spatula. As amateurs, we will have made sure that the larger, buttered skillet is hot but not smoking and will simply overturn the small skillet to drop the crêpe into the large one. Cook it about a minute and then lift it with a spatula or turner onto a plate. Repeat until you have about a dozen perfect crêpes. Some will probably be imperfect and be discarded. Cover the stack of pancakes with waxed paper. They will keep for about 12 hours.

One of our favorite food writers, James Beard, now reduces this recipe to its ultimate simplicity. He suggests that you now make any sweet soufflé and use it to stuff the crêpes. We like the following version:

3 tablespoons butter, preferably unsalted

5 tablespoons sifted flour

½ cup milk

3 large or 4 medium-to-small egg yolks (save 3 egg whites—they come later)

4 tablespoons sugar

1 tablespoon freshly grated peel of a lemon or lime

The juice of that lemon or lime, plus the juice of half another, strained

3 egg whites, the ones you reserved above

⅛ teaspoon salt

Heat the oven to 400 degrees (or simply raise it to that after you take out the Yorkshire pudding). In a saucepan, melt the butter, add the flour and, stirring with a whisk, cook about a minute and a half. Meanwhile, in another saucepan, heat the milk until quite hot but not boiling. Add it to the butter-flour mixture and cook until it begins to bubble and thickens. Remove from the heat and whip in the egg yolks, one at a time. Add 3 tablespoons of the sugar, the citrus juice and the peel, stirring thoroughly.

Whip the egg whites, salt and remaining sugar until the whites form steady peaks. Lightly fold a tablespoon of the three egg whites into the yolk mixture, then lightly and gently fold the yolk mixture into the whites.

Butter a large, shallow baking dish. On one half of each crêpe, place a tablespoon of the soufflé mixture; then fold over the other half; fold again to make a triangle, and place in the baking dish. Sprinkle with sugar—say a quarter of a teaspoon each, but don't take the time to measure—and bake 10 minutes or until the soufflé puffs up. Serve immediately.

What are the advantages of this menu?

—Only the crêpes are involved enough to give trouble to even the rankest beginner. A couple of our tricks, using the second skillet and pouring off the excess batter, should eliminate some early disasters with crêpes; these methods are aids-to-amateurs which we learned later.

—The beef entrée is calculated to please your meat-and-potatoes guests while the other dishes permit you to show off cooking skills.

—Much can be done ahead of time. There is only one brief time when both of you must be out of the dining room—while one clears the table of the main course dishes and assembles the salad from previously prepared components, the other can mix the soufflé and assemble the crêpes to stick in the oven halfway through the salad course.

—Two cooks working together can easily divide the chores between them according to their skills and preferences and, by doing so, have more combined time together with their guests.

2

Setting Up Housekeeping

**First mistakes, the search for fennel,
The Incredible Bean Dish and
something called Old Carrot Soup**

TOO MANY American girls have learned to do cakes and pies and not much else by the time they suddenly are faced with running a kitchen for their own households. Too many American men, if they cook at all, base their reputations on a few specialties—steaks, salads, one spaghetti recipe or the like.

Dining and dating together with good appetites in the better restaurants of a city such as Minneapolis is enough to scare the wits out of an unprepared prospective bride. A wedding trip including great restaurants in New York and New Orleans, as well as the unique features of Bahamian cuisine, may see her appetite fading as she watches the fervor with which a new husband stuffs himself and as she dreads the task of preparing a first meal.

The best answer is that both cook. Particularly if both are employed and if there are schedule conflicts, they will achieve more time together. Their skills may prove complementary, and eventually they will teach one another to cook.

This was our first menu at home:

Martinis (he)

Pickled Pork Chops (she)

Okra and Tomatoes (he)   Buttered Noodles (she)

Green Salad (he)

Coffee (she)

All these except the okra we still serve in much the same manner as we first prepared them.

Pickled Pork Chops for Two

2 thick loin chops or 4 thinner ones

½ cup red wine vinegar (more or less depending on size of chops and size of vessel in which marinated)

1 clove garlic, crushed

1 bay leaf

½ teaspoon fennel seeds

¼ teaspoon oregano

¼ teaspoon red pepper flakes, or to taste

Olive oil for frying

1 egg, beaten

3 or 4 slices white bread, trimmed of crust and torn by hand into crumbs (For this dish the fluffiness of larger crumbs makes the hand-torn ones preferable to store or blender varieties.)

Trim most of the fat from chops and slash remaining fat every inch with a knife. Into a shallow dish large enough to hold the chops, pour enough vinegar to come halfway up the chops and mix into it the garlic, fennel seeds, oregano and pepper. Add chops and marinate two to four hours, turning them every half-hour or so.

Lift the chops from the marinade and wipe with paper towels. If desired, sprinkle lightly with salt and *very* lightly with black pepper. Dip in beaten egg on both sides and then in crumbs, pressing lightly.

Heat a skillet and add enough olive oil to cover the bottom of 27 the pan. Brown both sides of chops quickly over high heat, then lower heat to moderate. Turn only once after browning or you will loosen the breading. Total cooking time for inch-thick chops is about 15 minutes, or until a probing knife discovers no pink in the thickest part.

Okra and Tomatoes

Fresh okra was not often available in the North when we first made this dish, so we used frozen. It surprised us that in our first meal at home we invented a recipe. (The cookbooks in which we would have found instructions had not yet been unpacked.) This gave us courage for future efforts.

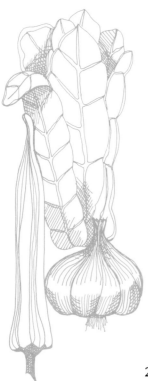

1 10-ounce package frozen whole okra

1 10½-ounce can whole-packed tomatoes

⅜ teaspoon dried basil

½ teaspoon vinegar or pickled pepper sauce

Salt and pepper to taste

Read the package instructions for the okra. From the liquid in which the tomatoes are packed, pour off as much as the amount of water needed to cook the okra; use this as your cooking liquid, adding water if necessary to make up the amount required.

Cook the okra about one minute *less* than the minimum time stated on the package, then add the tomatoes (which you've broken up with a fork), the basil, salt and pepper, and heat through to a simmer. Add the vinegar or pepper sauce and serve.

Buttered Noodles

We prefer Italian-style rather than German-style noodles, about 6 ounces for two persons. Cook to the minimum cooking time stated on package, drain and put immediately into a warm bowl in which half a stick of butter has been melting. Salt and heavily pepper and serve quickly with Parmesan cheese on the side.

Green Salad

We didn't know at the time that this was a good idea, but we try to have at least two and preferably three kinds of greens in our salads. In order of preference, our basic green is leaf lettuce, bibb, romaine or Boston lettuce. To the basic green, we add a smaller amount of watercress, endive or both; Belgian endive when in season, curly endive (also called chicory) when Belgian is not available. Exceptions are Greek salads, in which we use only chicory, and Caesar salads, in which we use only romaine.

We never use iceberg lettuce except (a) when there's no other usable looking green in the store, or (b) for certain very specialized Mexican or Italian salads in which the flavor of the dressing is the compelling thing, and the tasteless iceberg green is simply a flavor-carrier.

More later on salad dressings; we used a bottled dressing the first time out. Even then, however, we knew enough to avoid the "red" so-called French dressings; a true French dressing is clear. A bottled "Italian" dressing probably comes closer to French than anything except those bottled French dressings prepared by olive oil manufacturers.

Coffee

We prefer a drip pot, though like most people we received percolators as wedding gifts. Remember, however, that for American-style coffee, you should make the total capacity of the pot, not a partial pot, and that you should use one-sixth as much coffee as water. (This means two tablespoons, which is one ounce, per six-ounce coffee cup, or one six-ounce cup per six-cup pot. Remember also that "cup" in reference to coffee means six ounces volume, but that any measuring cup is calibrated in true eight-ounce cups.)

That first meal was edible, but we unpacked our few cookbooks the next day. (We include a chapter on cookbooks later.) The pickled pork chops had been practiced incessantly on the bride's family the 29 month before the wedding—but only after resolving one small hitch: she couldn't find fennel seeds in her small hometown and had to pick them up on her next trip to the city 100 miles away.

Other dishes that bailed us out early on were:

The Incredible Bean Dish

For some eight years, after a social disaster while entertaining with it, this was known as the Unfortunate Bean Dish. Boldly we tried it again, renamed it the Incredible Bean Dish, and have it two or three times a year, either en *famille* or for drop-in guests.

Saute a large chopped onion and one or two cloves of garlic in 3 or 4 tablespoons lard or cooking oil until just tender. Half a chopped green pepper may also be used with the onion. Add 2 cans of drained pinto or red kidney beans and half a bottle of red wine. Bring to a boil, then simmer for 10 minutes. Add 1½ cups of diced, cooked ham ("tenderized" or watered ham will do, but country ham is best), stir and simmer until heated through (about 15 minutes). Serve with plenty of bread for sopping.

Coarse as it is this dish still can make a reputation for a young cook—or a pair of them.

Eggs

Apart from the standard injunction that all eggs except those in an omelet should be cooked slowly, you can learn all you need to know about egg cookery from almost any cookbook. But there is one trick too often unmentioned which one of us, fortunately, already knew when we were married. If you find it odious or difficult to baste the top of an egg with fat while frying, and either don't like your egg flipped or lack the skill to flip it, try this:

Fry no more than three eggs per 10-inch skillet. Break each egg into an individual saucer or custard cup. Heat skillet over medium heat and add two tablespoons butter. When the butter starts to sizzle, reduce heat to low and slide each egg from its saucer, held at the center of the skillet, toward the outside of the skillet, thus keeping the whites separated. (You may need a knife or spatula to help keep the whites apart.) When whites begin to set, add 1 teaspoon of water per egg and immediately cover the skillet tightly. Cook a minute to a minute and a half more. The bottom of the egg is fried and the top is steamed, but it works, and no one will ever question you.

Having learned this technique, if you are a Rex Stout reader, you may immediately figure out your own recipe for Eggs Nero Wolfe. If not, here was our original solution to the mystery:

Proceed as above, but instead of adding water, add 2 teaspoons of good medium-dry sherry per egg, reduce heat to very low, cover and steam for 2 minutes. Serve topped with black butter. To make enough black butter for four eggs, use 2 tablespoons of butter and brown it very quickly in a separate, very hot skillet.

Like Stout's Inspector Cramer, we wound up with egg on our face. Since writing the above, we have seen the long-awaited *Nero Wolfe Cookbook,* prepared under Stout's supervision. The book's method is entirely different from ours, and the dish much more delicate. (We still like the method we invented from the brief description in *Over my Dead Body*.)

Stout would have you cook the eggs in baking cups, add a smaller quantity of sherry and then film the tops of the eggs under the broiler rather than by steaming. He suggests using clarified butter, described in the previous chapter, to make the "black" butter (actually brown) which goes over the eggs just before serving.

Old Carrot Soup

The name and the origin of this coarse but sometime useful throw-together lies with an earlier two in what can hardly be called a kitchen. Two students shared a dingy room in a dingy rooming house and cooked on a forbidden hotplate, storing their food under a wet towel in an open window in lieu of refrigeration.

When one returned from class in a rush during a one-hour lunch break, he found his roommate (now a professor of English at Wichita   31

State University) rifling drawers and bookcases and generally taking the place apart.

"What's up, Jim?"

"Where," replied Jim, "is that old carrot we used to have?"

You will need a package of dehydrated soup—chicken noodle or what have you. Chop two or three slices of bacon and fry with a chopped large onion in a large saucepan until onion is almost wilted. Add the amount of water called for on the soup package, bring to a boil and add the contents of the package. Add raw vegetables as desired, or add cooked leftover vegetables near the end of the package cooking time.

The carrot is optional. They never did find the damned thing.

Precocious Entertaining

**Cocktails for 30 after the opera and the
case against pheasant**

THE LIVING ROOM and bedroom of our first apartment were livable
enough, but the kitchen and dinette weren't big enough to make one
good dungeon cell. With more good spirit than good sense and only
about a month's real kitchen experience, we invited 30 people in for
drinks one Sunday afternoon—and got home from the opera half an
hour before the guests were due.

We purchased two dozen of the cheapest cocktail glasses we
could find (and were still using them six years later except for formal
occasions). The day before, we premixed, strained and stored in the
freezing compartment two quarts of martinis and a quart of manhat-
tans. We arranged for a particular friend to show up 10 minutes early
for the party with 20 pounds of ice cubes and five pounds of crushed
ice. Highball materials, sherry for the light drinkers, and tomato juice,
cola and ginger ale for the nondrinkers were at hand. All coffee pots
were loaded and on standby.

Mexican foods were not then so nationally known. One of us,
however, had memories of having seen New Yorkers so gorge themselves on slightly underseasoned *chili con queso* that they couldn't 33

do justice to the dinner that followed. We fried a large grocery bag of crisp tortillas the day before, to be heated briefly in the oven just before serving, and made the *chili con queso* Sunday morning to be warmed in a chafing dish just before the guests arrived.

Chili con Queso

To serve four to six as an appetizer or cocktail dip, chop coarsely one large onion and fry in 2 tablespoons butter until transparent. Add one 10-ounce can mixed tomatoes and green chili and bring to a simmer. (The dish is still better if, instead of the canned product, a large tomato, peeled and chopped, and a medium-sized, medium-hot chopped green chili are used. In this case, cook the tomato and chili with the onion for 8 to 10 minutes or until chili is tender.) Add ½ pound grated cheese: goat cheese, Monterrey Jack or mild cheddar. Stir until cheese melts and the other ingredients are well mixed; add salt to taste. Serve hot over crisp tortillas, or put in a chafing dish, its heat low, with tortillas on the side for dipping.

Despite the opera tickets, we thought we'd try to make guacamole salad. Though its remains had turned dark green (and thus bad) before the last guests arrived, most of it had been eaten long before, and we had discovered a way of pre-preparing this highly perishable dish to keep it for several hours.

There are literally dozens of recipes for guacamole, and it tastes a little different every time we make it. The following is merely an approximation of what we did the last time we made it, plus instructions for keeping it.

Guacamole

To serve four to six as a salad or cocktail dip, chop a small onion and a peeled, medium-sized tomato. Add a chopped, medium-hot green chili or a tablespoon of chili powder. With a fork, mash into this mixture the meat of two large, dead-ripe (soft) avocados. (If you don't overdo it, an electric mixer does this quickly; the avocado 34 should remain a little lumpy.) Add 2 or more tablespoons of homemade French or bottled Italian dressing. Mix and correct seasonings.

If you wish to keep the guacamole a few hours before serving, drop the avocado pits on top of it. (This probably doesn't do any good, but it's supposed to slow the spoilage of the avocado meat.) Probably more effective: use a tablespoon less of the salad dressing than your taste dictates, then use a teaspoon of the salad dressing to thin a tablespoon of mayonnaise. Smooth the surface of the guacamole (except where the pit protrudes) and spread the mayonnaise mixture over it in as nearly airtight a thin coating as you can. Refrigerate. Just before serving, remove and discard the pits, mix the mayonnaise film into the salad and add a garnish if desired. (Garnish may be chopped nuts, crisp, crumbled bacon bits, or finely chopped fresh cilantro leaves.)

An aphorism not coined by that well-fed but pompous Frenchman Brillat-Savarin: when an avocado salad turns avocado-colored, it's gone bad.

We completed the cocktail edibles with a large bowl of *les crudités*—raw vegetables such as scallions, celery, carrot sticks and the like. In our inexperience, we used a smaller variety of vegetables and a less distinguished dip sauce than is suggested in a later chapter, "The Unexpected Vegetable."

Because the guests were newspaper folk, some of whom work days and some of whom work nights, it was necessary to keep the bar and board open some eight hours. No one except the hosts, however, stayed too long, and the hosts had taken a precaution: mixed and camouflaged in the refrigerator were two quarts of iced coffee which we sipped over ice (from an opaque highball glass) about every other drink.

Not even the landlord complained, and we were launched as hosts with an enviable if as yet unearned reputation.

The reputation we earned the next few months was less enviable. We served a delicious but unseasonable lasagna to an ill-assorted group of guests in an unairconditioned apartment in the heat of sum- 35 mer. We had too many planter's punches both before and after taking one of our wedding ushers to a baseball game (which the home team lost) and grew heads the size of basketballs.

And then there was the pheasant. With more money than brains, we bought frozen pheasant and put on a three-wine, multi-course dinner for people we particularly wanted to impress. Among other disasters, the pheasant was too old (thus tough) for the cooking method we used; the guests were grimly polite, and most of the pheasant went into the incinerator at midnight with the only laugh of the evening: "We have the most expensive garbage in town."

From that experience came a lesson we suggest to you: particularly when entertaining, try cooking things only a *little* more difficult than you know you can do. Soon you'll be serving Beef Wellington.

When we left that apartment for our first house, we quickly acquired our first charcoal grill. The first things cooked on it, spareribs and roast corn, have become the entire family's favorite summer menu. When daughter No. 1 shed her dental braces, it became the entrée for the celebration featuring all the things she hadn't been permitted to eat for 15 months. Although the sparerib recipe we first used came from a cookbook, it's been altered over the years to approximate the spareribs served in the 50s at the Uptown Pit Barbecue in Oklahoma City, simply the greatest ever barbecued. The taste of the finished product is surprisingly more delicate than the amount of garlic and spices might suggest.

Spareribs Oklahoma

4 pound strip spareribs
About 5 large cloves garlic, enough to make a tablespoon of
   pulp when crushed in a garlic press
1 tablespoon or more curry powder
2 tablespoons bottled onion juice
Basting sauce (see below)

36   Make a paste of the crushed garlic, curry powder and enough

Spareribs and roast corn have become the entire family's favorite summer menu. When daughter No. 1 shed her dental braces, it became the entreé for the celebration featuring all the things she hadn't been permitted to eat for 15 months.

Photos by Linda Wheeler for *The Washington Post*, by permission.

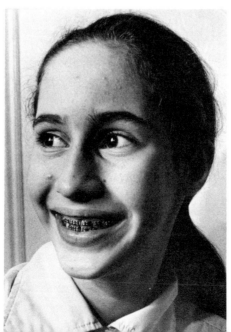

onion juice to get a spreadable consistency. Spread both sides of the ribs with it and let sit three hours or so, turning occasionally.

About an hour before dinner, start a good charcoal fire using enough briquets to spread them about an inch apart under the ribs and an inch outside the area the ribs take up on the grill. If you're going to do corn on the grill (it can go in the oven instead), the charcoal under the corn should be more closely distributed for higher heat.

Mix the following for a basting sauce:

1 8-ounce can tomato sauce

1 12-ounce can ale

1 tablespoon or more chili powder, preferably Gebhardt's

1 teaspoon ground ginger

½ teaspoon ground cumin

½ teaspoon dried rosemary (or, if you prefer, 1 teaspoon oregano—either herb should be crumbled with fingers or pestle)

1 teaspoon salt

Simmer the sauce five minutes to blend flavors.

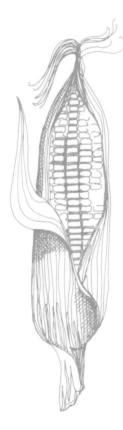

Cook the ribs slowly over charcoal, standing by with a child's water gun to shoot out flareups from the fat. Turn and baste about every five minutes. Check for doneness in about 25 minutes; it's usually 30 or 35 minutes before the last trace of pink disappears (as it must) from the thickest part of the meat.

If desired, bring the ribs near the coals for one minute per side to crisp the basting sauce that's adhering to them. This recipe serves four large or six medium appetites.

Roast Corn

You can clean your corn, butter it, add salt, pepper and herbs if desired, then wrap each ear in aluminum foil before cooking. But we find the best herbal flavor corn can get comes from the corn husks. 38 Either method works as well in an oven as on the grill.

Gently pull back the husks as far as they will go without breaking. Remove what silk you can and break or cut off the immature tip of the ear. Leaving husks rolled back, soak the corn in salt water (a teaspoon per quart) about half an hour. Then shake off excess water and carefully move the husks back into their original position around the corn.

Either roast in a 400-degree oven 20 to 25 minutes or place over high charcoal heat 20 minutes. (If over charcoal, give each ear a quarter turn every 5 minutes.) If served outdoors, leave the husks on for each diner to remove. Have soft butter, salt and a peppermill close at hand.

Cabbage Salad

Shred half a head of cabbage, preferably red.

Cut four slices of bacon into one-inch squares and fry crisp, reserving the fat. Return fat to skillet while bacon drains on absorbent paper. Add 2 tablespoons coarsely chopped onion, brown slowly, then remove with a slotted spoon and discard. Add 1½ tablespoons wine vinegar, salt and freshly ground pepper to taste. Bring just to a boil, pour over cabbage and toss, and place the bacon squares over the salad.

If you've bought the ribs but it rains too much to barbecue, make Chinese ribs in the oven instead of Oklahoma ribs outdoors.

Chinese Ribs

4 pounds baby strip spareribs
4 scallions cut in 2-inch pieces, including tops
3 cloves garlic mashed with flat of knife
4 tablespoons chili sauce
2 tablespoons ketchup
¼ cup soy sauce, preferably Chinese
¼ cup Chinese rice wine or dry sherry

2 tablespoons of corn syrup and 2 tablespoons honey
   (or use ¼ cup of either)
1 teaspoon salt
2 or more S-hooks for *each* piece of meat (use curtain hooks
   or bend 4-inch pieces of unpainted coat-hanger wire into
   S-shape with pliers)

Insert S-hooks into ribs so that each piece can hang (ribs vertical) from an oven rack while cooking. Lay ribs flat in a pan or dish, propping the hooks outside. Mix other ingredients and pour over ribs. Marinate at least three hours at room temperature, turning occasionally.

Move the top rack of your oven to highest position; move bottom rack to lowest or remove it. On bottom rack or on floor of the oven, place a large flat pan of cool water to catch fat and keep the humidity high. Preheat oven to 300 degrees.

Hang the ribs from the top rack of the oven, directly over the pan of water, with bones vertical. Cook for one hour at 300 degrees, then for 10 minutes at 425 degrees. Cut into individual ribs and, if you desire to crisp the adhering marinade, place ribs under the broiler for just a minute. Serve with plum sauce and hot mustard as an appetizer or main course.

Plum sauce, available from Chinese stores or international food shops, is spiced with chili peppers and garlic and is stronger in flavor than the sweet sauce served in most Chinese restaurants. Store leftover sauce in a tightly covered jar in the refrigerator; it will keep for several weeks. Mix hot mustard fresh (dry mustard and enough ice water to make it the consistency of heavy cream) and permit to stand for 10 minutes before serving. A recipe for Texas pecan pie, ideal dessert for a ribs-and-corn menu, appears on page 121.

This menu is so redundant with finger food of the greasiest sort that, in addition to a cloth napkin if you choose to use one, each

diner should have four or five paper napkins and, perhaps, a finger bowl. (Rough wooden or plastic finger bowls seem less ostentatious, and a wedge of lime instead of lemon in the warm water is a nice variation.) One ordinarily suave guest, a distinguished science writer, took half a dozen bites of such a dinner and proclaimed: "I haven't used a fork yet, and I don't think I shall!"

4

Cookbooks:
Their Uses and Abuses

**Or how Betty Crocker wed Escoffier
on Christmas Day in the morning**

IN THEORY, after a few years' careful practice and thought about cooking, you should never need to use a recipe. Your tongue, nose and brain will be trained to recognize and duplicate tastes; your knowledge of cooking techniques will tell you instantly what process was used to create a dish you admire, and your imagination will enable you to improve it. Although your greatest adventures in cooking may come from things you've eaten, you'll want a map to guide you along some of these roads.

Presumably you own at least one all-purpose cookbook. If it's a good and generalized one, like *The New York Times Cookbook,* you may go a long time before buying another (though perhaps you won't when you learn that cookbooks can be fun to read). But if your book is overly cutesy, or you find things made by the book's recipes universally bland, or every cooking times seems to be either inexact or incorrect, make room on the shelf for a better one.

Of at least a hundred kitchen books we've acquired over 17 years, perhaps 20 are of so little value that they may go years at a time without use for so much as a reference, much less a recipe. Others are so specialized or opinionated that they're rarely used except as references. A few, though useful to read, are written on a professional level beyond the capabilities of our kitchen. A few we've simply outgrown—but remembering a great dinner from years before may send us back to one of them.

At menu-planning time, each of us may sit with a drink at one elbow and a stack of cookbooks at the other, calling out ideas to one another and, not infrequently, finding ideas for original dishes from the suggestions of not-quite-satisfactory recipes. Eventually, with courage and any palate at all, you should be able to judge most recipes merely by reading them without having to cook them.

If you're really a beginner, and perhaps if you are not, you can do worse than to start with a textbook. We bought *Craig Claiborne's Kitchen Primer* a few years ago as a gift for an 11-year-old girl who was just getting interested in cooking. We quickly learned that some of the techniques he teaches beginners were more efficient than techniques we had refined to a nicety through years of experience.

A mainstay in our kitchen is our assortment of books both hardbound and paperback, both all-purpose and specialized, by James Beard. They require some enjoyable getting to know. Yet, we've never owned a book of his that doesn't show many proud stains of kitchen usage. Smokers, in particular, find the additional seasonings in some of his recipes get through to tar-coated palates (Worcestershire sauce in Steak Diane, for example). But delicacy is not forgotten; we've read no other writer who points out that true tartar sauce is basically quiet, made with shallots and clipped fresh dill, rather than the usual onions and dill pickle. Beard frequently leaves leeway for the cook's imagination. This should not alarm the beginner; if you don't think you have the feel for choosing a particular amount or using the suggested technique, simply cross-check with another book.

If you insist upon very exact measurements, precision in the ingredients list was invented by Fanny Farmer in 1896 and, years after 43 that lady's death, the books bearing her name continue it. For absolute precision in describing techniques, there's Julia Child, but her books come closer to textbook than to all-purpose cookbook.

Specialized cookbooks fall into several subsections—national, regional and product.

Because one of our tricks in the creation of a distinctive family cuisine is the occasional inclusion of one or more ethnic dishes in a well-planned meal, we'd argue strongly for at least one good national cookbook from each of at least the following cuisines: Chinese, Italian, Hungarian, Spanish and Mexican. In your first ventures, try to buy fairly simple ones—Grace Zia Chu's *The Pleasures of Chinese Cooking,* for example, is dependable, simple and precise in its instructions. It can give you many hours and months of cooking pleasure before you will want to move on to a work more encyclopedic.

Regional cookbooks can be good or bad—beware of those in which most recipes are signed by some unknown person from Splitlip, U.S.A. Many of these recipes, depending on the book, may not have been test-cooked by the compiler's staff, and unless the book indicates test-cooking has been done, you'll wind up correcting the recipes yourself.

Product cookbooks—recipes featuring beer, coffee, sausage or what have you—can contain many good and many bad ideas (and in some cases be subsidized by a maker of the product featured or by a trade association). The best product book we know, *Pasta* by Jack Denton Scott, is almost a generalized Italian national cookbook. It also offers a good example of how to treat a paperback cookbook. Since we never have encountered the $15 hard-bound version, when we found the 95-cent paperback so useful we bought eight copies of it. Once or twice when a guest was unusually impressed by a dish created from it, we simply gave the guest a copy of the book. And we've never had to hold a copy together with a rubber band, as is so often the case with a frequently used paperback cookbook.

44   You will also need a good reference book on potables and drink

recipes. Though perhaps a little out of date and originally intended as a professional reference book, we're proud to own and use *Grossman's Guide to Wines, Spirits and Beers.*

Books about food include, like this book, more discourse on food than recipes. The acknowledged classic in the field is Professor Saintsbury's *Notes on a Cellar Book,* of which we'd heard for years before spotting a copy in a second-hand bookstore. Modern mistress of the field is M.F.K. Fisher, five of whose books have been published in one volume as *The Art of Eating.*

Memory doesn't reveal whether it was through whim or fancy that we bought the American version of *The Escoffier Cook Book.* But even in the home kitchen, it proves useful as a reference work which may help you perfect lesser recipes. And it was directly responsible many years ago for getting us to the end of one of our first clumsy but successful efforts at a holiday menu.

Plum Pudding Crocker-Escoffier

We wanted plum pudding, yet were dissatisfied with the recipes we had available. In desperation we checked Escoffier; his recipe sounded right, but the proportions were enough to feed a cavalry troop (including horses) and the amounts were specified in weights for which we didn't have a kitchen scale. While starting laboriously to work out the pounds into cups and tablespoons, memory tickled: This recipe was almost exactly like the one given in *Betty Crocker's Picture Cook Book,* except that the fictitious Ms. Crocker had taken the booze out of the batter, substituting fruit juice. Wedding her work with Escoffier's (and, after experimenting, adding the candied ginger as our own idea) we produced the recipe we still use today:

    ½ pound ground suet

    1½ cups bread crumbs

    1 cup flour, sifted with:

        1 teaspoon soda

        1 teaspoon salt

1 teaspoon cinnamon

¼ teaspoon nutmeg

¾ teaspoon mace

1 cup peeled and chopped apple

1 cup each dark raisins, sultanas and currants

2 tablespoons each chopped, all candied, orange, lemon, citron peel and ginger

½ cup chopped English Walnuts

1 cup brown sugar (Escoffier used confectioner's sugar.)

Juice and chopped peel of half a lemon and a quarter of an orange

2 eggs, beaten

2 ounces rum or brandy, plus 1½ ounces for flaming

3 ounces stout

6 tablespoons currant jelly

If there is time, soak the fruits in rum or brandy a day or two before cooking. Mix all ingredients together (except the last 1½ ounces of spirits) and pour into a greased 2-quart, tube center pudding mold (with locking cover). Cover, place on rack in large kettle with enough boiling water to come halfway up the mold and steam for six hours, replenishing water as needed.

Unmold onto serving plate and, naturally, pour over and ignite 1½ ounces of heated brandy or rum. Pass the chilled hard sauce (1 cup soft butter creamed with 1½ cups sifted confectioner's sugar) and an ounce of rum, brandy or Grand Marnier.

Restaurants: Their Lessons

What restaurants teach you rates them almost as well as what they feed you

THOUGH YOU MAY NEVER completely reach the happy state of cooking entirely without recipes—we certainly haven't—you still can duplicate approximately 80 percent of the new dishes you encounter. You must think carefully about the tastes even as you eat and remember them later as you strive to match or improve them. True taste memory in a cook has been likened to absolute pitch in a musician, a talent few have been blessed with. But *relative* pitch can take a musician a long way, and everyone who knows an apple from an onion has, and can develop further, relative taste memory.

And who better to imitate than the best professionals. Though some restaurants cling to the mystique of "secret" recipes, many chefs—and waiters—are so proud to see their work thoughtfully admired that they will share a recipe with you. If they will not, simply work it out for yourself.

Here are some restaurant-experiences that have broadened the repertoire of our kitchen. If Minneapolis seems overrepresented, 47 there is a very good reason: for a midwestern city, it is a far better than average restaurant town. And we first started teaching one another to cook while we lived there.

Harry's Cafe Superieur, Minneapolis, is basically just a big, gracious beef and lobster house, sprawled on three levels of a converted old downtown home with a rickety elevator. But the martinis are crisp and frigid, and with them are served such memorable popovers that you easily could kill your appetite for the tremendous steak to follow. After a few such dinners, we bought a good, cast-iron popover pan and tried to make our own. Result: puddles. Noting our admiration for popovers, a waiter at Harry's asked if we made our own.

"Only failures," one of us replied.

"Well, here's the secret," said the waiter. "Take any standard popover recipe. Use one more egg. Then, when it calls for milk, use half milk and half water."

We've never had a failure since. The recipe, as corrected by our waiter's advice, comes out thus:

Harry's Popovers

Grease popover pan and let it heat in oven as oven warms to 425 degrees. Beat together until just smooth:

1 cup sifted flour

½ teaspoon salt

½ cup water

½ cup milk

3 eggs

Fill the popover iron three-quarters full and bake 35 to 45 minutes, until popovers are high and golden brown.

Chateau de Paris in the Hotel Dyckman, Minneapolis, introduced many midwesterners to their first truly classic French cooking and quietly spectacular service. We first encountered the lamb chops with six or more vegetables, described in the later chapter "You Can't 48 Go It Alone," when the Chateau was still a small, bright, austerely elegant room behind the bar, not the plush, dim, giant establishment it since has become.

You've probably heard that the young prefer Burgundy and learn to appreciate and finally prefer Bordeaux as they grow older. For us, age brought an increased appreciation of tarragon, an herb that struck our young palates as unpleasantly sweet. Learning to appreciate tarragon and trusting whatever taste memory we have, enabled us to approximate the salad dressing we so much enjoyed at Chateau de Paris in the 1950s. We knew it was basically a thin mayonnaise, we finally discovered the need for chervil, but until we doubled the amount of tarragon, the taste never seemed quite right. This is how we make it today:

In a blender, place a well-minced clove of garlic, an egg yolk, half a teaspoon each of salt and dry mustard, a quarter teaspoon each of dry basil and chervil, almost a half teaspoon of tarragon, an eighth teaspoon of cayenne (or less), and two tablespoons mild wine vinegar. (If your vinegar is too strong, diluting it with water will work better than adding sugar.) Blend quickly; then, with blender still running, add slowly ¾ cup of half peanut oil and half olive oil. Add two more tablespoons of vinegar, mix and age several hours in the refrigerator.

When added to a mixture of greens which is about half leaf lettuce and a quarter each endive and watercress, this dressing produces Salade Jeanne—not something we actually ate at Chateau de Paris but based on tastes acquired there. Wash, chill and dry the greens; use only enough of the dressing to moisten them as you toss the salad. The remaining dressing, covered, will keep in the refrigerator for up to two days.

The Old Ebbitt Grill in Washington has to be discussed as the "old" Old Ebbitt and the "new" Old Ebbitt. In the old place, the plain, hearty food was distinguished by the brusque service of ancient but nonsubservient black waiters and the house's own musty ale on draught. To the sorrow of thousands, it went broke after a hundred years or so.

Reopened in the same old hall under new management, the "new" Ebbitt lacks the ale, and the waiters are younger and more polite, but the food continues to be memorable. Especially outstanding is one occasional soup which we duplicated thus:

Cabbage Ebbitt

Reheat 3 cups of the beef-tomato soup described in "The Non-convenience Foods" (page 113). While the soup heats, cut a quarter of a small cabbage into bite-sized pieces and parboil in salted water until almost tender but still chewy (about 3 minutes). Drain and add to the soup. Serves six.

Ristorante La Scala in New York is not the finest Italian restuarant we know, merely our favorite. Though the food can be surpassed, the charm of La Scala's proprietor-hosts cannot; their graciousness toward any presentable stranger equals that shown to their oldest customers.

Yet there are some strange things about La Scala. It is a house rule, for example, that no dish ever contains both garlic and onions—a purism that few kitchens would want to adopt. Much more acceptable, especially to people who are traditionalists about birthdays but really don't like cake, are the miniature rum cakes served to birthday guests.

We almost accidentally created a dish reminiscent of La Scala's cuisine, although we cannot recall ever having had it there in exactly this form:

Peppers and Mushrooms

3 large or 4 small sweet peppers, green or both red and green
2 cloves garlic
¼ cup olive oil
¼ cup butter
½ pound mushrooms, about 1-inch caps
Salt and pepper

½ teaspoon dried oregano

Remove seeds and ribs from peppers and cut peppers into eighths. In a skillet for which you have a lid, melt the butter in the olive oil over medium heat. Cut peeled garlic cloves in half lengthwise. When foam subsides in the skillet, brown the garlic, then remove and discard. Add the peppers, cover, reduce heat to low, and cook until tender (about 20 minutes), stirring occasionally.

Meanwhile, clean the mushrooms and cut into halves or quarters vertically. Add to the peppers and cook about five minutes more, stirring once or twice. Season with salt and pepper to taste and sprinkle with oregano, rubbing it between your palms. Stir and serve as a side dish with steak or mixed Italian sausages.

The Northern Pacific railroad is no more, and Amtrak's trains no longer stop at Little Falls, Minnesota. When they did, our weekend trips there featured a baby in a basket and breakfast in the diner. Several years ago, while the train still ran, that sometime baby accompanied her parents and a younger sister on a frustrating, sentimental repeat of that train ride. The crisp linens and shining silver of the diner had been replaced by chrome and plastic; the waiter's "May I help you, sir?" had become, in the cafeteria line, "Yeah, buddy, what's yours?" In memory of the trains of yesteryear, we recreated upon returning home our favorite railroad breakfast dish.

Omelet Northern Pacific
2 dozen tiny button mushrooms or a dozen medium mushrooms
¾ cup mixed olive and peanut oil
¼ cup white wine vinegar
½ teaspoon salt
¼ teaspoon dry mustard
Few grinds black pepper
6 to 8 eggs for omelets
Butter, water, salt and pepper for omelet
With button mushrooms, cut the stems off even with the bottom of the cap; with larger mushrooms, slice thinly, cutting vertically   51

through both stem and cap at the stem area. Mix the oils, vinegar and spices and pour over the mushrooms in a shallow dish. Marinate half an hour.

Make three or four individual French omelets (for technique, see page 125, "What to Cook When There's Nothing to Eat in the House"). Arrange drained mushrooms over the omelets before folding, and serve with crisp bacon and a garnish of parsley.

6

Shoulder to Shoulder

**Or, dammit, don't get bolder when I'm using a knife;
a guide to ifs, ands, pots and pans in a small kitchen**

WHEN HE GETS TO THE KITCHEN of an apartment or small house, it seems the architect usually resigns. A descendant of the Marquis de Sade, previously employed as a sardine packer, replaces him as creator of the culinary areas of your home.

Particularly if your team of two is just starting out, there will be barely room for one in the kitchen. You may wind up preparing alternate meals (he gets lunch while she plans dinner) or else you'll be bumbling around the kitchen jovially (we hope) but inefficiently.

Craig Claiborne says in his *Kitchen Primer* (and if we had to, we'd trade one of his seven or more fine books for this one sentence): ". . . the most important thing in learning to cook well and with love is a sense of organization." That, of course, involves having ingredients premeasured or standing by readily measurable, and planning out the menu so carefully that the various chores are fairly divided between the co-chefs. 53

Most important is organizing your space. After 17 years, we still work together successfully in a kitchen with available floor space only about 3 by 12 feet and counter space totalling only about 12 square feet. By long habit, the one who has to do the heaviest chopping uses the cabinet with the chopping-block top; the other goes to the other end of the room. Each uses the side of the stove nearer his own working area. When one needs something from the cabinet over which his partner is working, he quickly checks what he's interrupting before plunging in.

Working together requires courtesy, love and a kind of telepathy. When you spoil a dish or do something plain stupid, some of your worst quarrels are likely to occur. Among the things we've learned for preservation of a marriage:

• Don't get unexpectedly affectionate when your partner is hard at work with a knife; he's more likely to cut himself than you.

• Never, never (unless asked) take over a dish from your partner; better to eat a bad job than to eat with the bad appetite of a quarrel. Most often, your uninvited expertise will mess up the dish rather than help it.

• Particularly if you have only a single oven, plan together when, how and at what temperature it will be used. You'll hardly be able to steam a Smithfield ham the same night your partner wants to do a cheese cake.

• Learn to laugh at disasters.

What kitchen equipment to buy? Many good cookbooks offer lists of first purchase and second purchase "necessary" equipment; these lists are usually good and sound, but we think they miss two points:

• Although equipping a new kitchen can be a major financial investment, space may be even more important. "What can we store?" may be an even more important question than "What can we afford?"

• Particularly for those who choose to cook *a deux*, many purchases and gifts of the past may have to be lived with; you don't throw out Great-Aunt Bertha's frying pan until either she or it dies.

First you need to plan storage space. Can you mount pegboards in or near the kitchen to multiply your space for pots and pans? (We sealed off an unneeded doorway between our living room and a kitchen hallway, creating a space for a needed bookcase on the living room side and a pegboard for kitchen utensils on the other. We also put another pegboard at the other end of the kitchen.) Can you tastefully mount a bookcase in your dining area to carry your cookbooks? Do you have storage space in a basement, pantry or closet for specialty items that you use only every month or so—a noodle machine, a spaetzle machine, a chafing dish?

After you discover how much you can store, take a good equipment list and adapt it to your needs, or make your own. Here are a few of the points we would consider:

• If you're not awfully fond of cakes and pies, skip buying these pans until you need them. Or, if you expect to have a larger kitchen in a year or so, use disposable foil pans—less satisfactory but passable.

• Check whatever covers might fit your skillets before buying separate covers for them. (The cover of our Dutch oven fits the twelve-inch skillet, the cover of a small soup pot fits the ten-inch, we don't have an eight-inch and the cover of the double boiler fits the six-inch.)

• Gifts and leftovers from bachelor days may determine the material for your saucepans and kettles. If you have a choice, we'd vote for copper-bound stainless steel for durability. Enamel-coated cast iron may cook better but doesn't last as long. Aluminum discolors some food. But try to live with what you have until it wears out; then you will have your own opinions on replacements.

• If your basic cutlery is stainless steel, you will need an electric knife sharpener unless you're lucky enough to live in a neighborhood like ours where the grindstone man still comes around, wheel on his back. If you're lucky enough to be given or can afford really good 55

carbon steel cutlery, you can keep it to a fine edge by hand with very little trouble. But remember you also will need a couple of stainless steel blades for cutting onions and acidulous fruits, which will discolor and be discolored by the carbon steel of the finer blades.

• The same experts who say you need a set of graduated, metal measuring cups for measuring solids also say that exactitude of measurement is rarely that important. If space is at a premium, you *can* measure solids with the glass measuring cups you use for liquids.

• Buy a spice rack at least three times larger than you expect to need; if you really like variety in eating, your spices will proliferate fantastically.

• When picking a corkscrew, take some time to find one with a flat blade, not just wire. Contrary to popular superstition, the new gas-powered cork pullers do not damage wine—but they do sometimes open the bottle so explosively that the wine damages clothing and linens. Your can opener, beer opener and corkscrew should be three separate implements, not a combination job.

• For two in the kitchen, some of your smaller implements such as the swivel-bladed knife (peeler) should be bought two at a time: one for each.

• Though rarely listed as necessary equipment, a grapefruit knife is useful even for people who hate grapefruit. It has a double-edged, serrated blade, curving at the tip, and is helpful in trimming every fruit from peaches to pineapples.

• We would urge even beginners to get and use a *choy doh,* the cleaver-shaped Chinese knife. With it buy a Chinese cookbook which includes a chapter on how to use the knife; read the chapter before taking the knife out of its wrapping. Properly used, the *choy doh* is safe and a work-saver in *all* cuisines including the French. It can be used for cleaving, cutting, chopping, crushing and carrying food from cutting block to cooking vessel; in some dishes, a single *choy doh* may serve all five purposes. Though it may not be so pretty, treat it like the finest carbon steel. 57

Pegboards in or near the kitchen multiply your space for pots and pans.

As for electrical appliances, the one you probably need least is a coffee maker. (We prefer a plain drip pot.) In deciding what the budget will stand (or what to get when trading in duplicated wedding gifts), first consider these:

• An electric blender has become almost a necessity in the modern kitchen; it permits doing in seconds jobs that once took hours or didn't get done at all.

• An electric skillet provides controlled heat for long frying jobs and frees stove-top space. Also, if the controls are attached to the cord rather than the skillet, it can be cleaned, unlike your good cast-iron skillet, in an automatic dishwasher.

• An electric mixer seems essential unless you want to spend inordinate minutes beating egg whites and the like by hand. If you have the space, a standing model will do jobs the more convenient hand-held model cannot.

• An electric meat grinder is needed for meats contemporary butchers refuse to grind such as pork and suet. And for some dishes such as Steak Tartare, meat should be ground as soon before serving as possible for both health and taste reasons.

• An electric ice crusher is useful for drinks both alcoholic and non. You can try your blender, but most make mushed ice, not crushed.

If your first apartment is in an older building, find out how modern the wiring is. We once blew the fuses nine minutes before guests were due by using an electric skillet and coffee maker at the same time.

Probably you will have whatever kind of range the landlord prefers and won't have to get into the decades-old controversy between electricity and gas. We do find gas heat better for stove-top cooking and broiling; electric heat somewhat better for baking, particularly if the oven has all the modern automatic devices.

If we ever build our dream kitchen, it will have a combination stove: gas burners, with their quick-change heat control; an electric 59

Buy a spice rack at least three times as large as you think you'll need.

deep-well cooker for deep frying and soups; two ovens, one gas and one electric. And a well-vented fireplace, with a spit!

Finally, have a long, sensible smock or apron for each cook.

An Alternative to Pro Football

Some notions on Sunday brunch

SOMEWHERE BETWEEN eggs and bacon and soup and salad is the meal known as brunch. As a way to spend a good portion of a Sunday afternoon with friends, it even rivals football watching. But if it's New Year's Day or Super Bowl Day, you had best offer to substitute the television set for conversation.

The dictionary defines brunch as "a late breakfast, an early lunch, or a combination of the two." Following the last definition produces the most satisfying results for hosts and guests alike. Here are two menus featuring dressed-up versions of the traditional ham-and-eggs breakfast:

The first is particularly well-suited to a picnic. Begin with a thermos of Bloody Marys (see page 132, "The Drinker's Dilemma"). Proceed with Oeufs Mollet, a kind of soft-boiled egg that can be served cold. To prepare them, bring water to a rolling boil; add eggs gently; immediately lower heat as much as possible. On a gas stove, that's just above the point where the flame goes out. If you are using an electric stove, have a heating unit ready on "warm" and switch the 61

pan to it as soon as you have added the eggs. Set the timer at six minutes. When the timer rings, immediately run the eggs under a heavy stream of cold tap water. Tuck into an egg carton for easy transportation. For easiest eating, cut off the very top of the shell with egg shears or a sharp knife, and eat right out of it. Demitasse spoons are good for this. And don't forget the peppermill.

The ham part of the menu appears as thin slices of prosciutto, wrapped around peeled wedges of cantaloupe or honeydew melon. Accompany with lime slices. As a finishing touch, serve strawberry muffins. Use any standard sweet muffin mix or recipe; fold in one cup of diced, well-drained strawberries for each dozen muffins. Iced coffee is a good choice as the beverage. Take chilled double-strength coffee in a thermos. Carry the ice (preferably crushed or chipped) separately.

The next menu also makes a good summer choice. But don't take it on a picnic unless you want to induce food poisoning. It's built around stuffed eggs, and their yolk and mayonnaise base makes them natural candidates for air-conditioned surroundings.

To have this dish come out satisfactorily, with a minimum of lumps, the eggs must not be overdone. We bring water to a full boil, add eggs and cook at a low simmer for 13 minutes. Immediately put the eggs under a stream of cold water. Split the hard-cooked eggs when cool and scoop the yolks into a bowl. Mash with a fork. Mix mayonnaise with enough fresh lemon juice to add tang. The consistency should be creamy. Combine this mixture with the yolks, stirring vigorously with a whisk. Add salt and pepper to taste.

Now comes the fun. Have as many large custard cups or small bowls ready as you want kinds of eggs. Divide the yolk mixture equally among the cups. Let your imagination play with different possibilities for spicing up the stuffings. Here are six ideas for a starting point. Assuming you had a dozen hard-cooked eggs, try these proportions:

62   To one dish add ¾ teaspoon chopped capers.

To the next, the crumbled bits from one slice of crisp bacon.

Then, ¾ teaspoon finely chopped peanuts.

Next, ½ teaspoon or more curry powder.

Again, 1 teaspoon or more of minced green onion, including the green part.

Finally, 2 dashes of Tabasco. Taste and, if that's not enough, add more.

Now stuff the whites with your six mixtures, and you will have an egg platter that puts the old deviled variety to shame.

To present the ham, first make small baking powder biscuits. Despite our usual purism, we find a mix does nicely. Cut the biscuits 1½ to 2 inches in diameter. (If you don't have a biscuit cutter, use the rim of a juice glass.) Split and butter them while still warm from the oven. Into each put a small slice of Smithfield or other country ham, fried or baked. Top with a smear of Dijon or other sharp prepared mustard.

A beverage of half V-8 juice and half beef bouillon, served on the rocks, complements this menu. (It's good in winter, too, drunk hot from mugs.) Fresh blueberries served with a sprinkling of kirsch make a pleasant final course.

Don't be afraid to build a brunch menu around a dish that usually makes its appearance at dinner. For example, start with two Chinese dishes described in other chapters: Szechuan duck, page 87, and Asparagus East, page 21. If desired, add scrambled eggs and the best brioche available, fresh or frozen. Complete the meal with a compote of stewed dry fruits, flavored with cinnamon, curry powder or allspice, as you choose.

Or, build a brunch menu around the delicate flavor of finnan haddie. Poach the fish gently in water or milk until it flakes easily with a fork. Drench with melted butter. Accompany with a scoop of cottage cheese with chives. The flavor of oats goes particularly well with this combination. Serve oat bread, muffins or cakes with butter and thyme honey.

We usually consider brunch entertaining more economical than   63 dinner or luncheon affairs. The following menu is a notable exception. But if you find your wallet full, few meals are more fun to prepare or more pleasing to guests.

The idea is to provide a groaning board filled with everything that usually makes its appearance at midnight snacks. Select a store that has as fine a variety of tinned delicacies, smoked fish and cheeses as possible. If you don't live near a city, take advantage of the many firms that sell such items by mail. Manganaro Foods, at 488 Ninth Avenue in New York, offers a particularly wide assortment.

Start with a routine item, a roasted fowl served at room temperature. Your bird may be the humble chicken, or perhaps a capon or goose. Substitute for dressing a stuffing of chunks of celery, onion and apple or pear. Use as much, packed loosely, as the bird will hold. This will impart a delicate flavor and help maintain shape while roasting, but it's not for consumption. Be sure the skin is crisp, to aid both taste and appearance.

Buy several varieties of smoked fish. The selection might include whitefish, lox and eel. Add some pickled herring for good measure. Include at least two kinds of cheese. A Canadian cheddar and a Cheshire would do nicely. Serve with a tray of black rye bread, in small rounds if possible. Accompany with a pot of whipped butter. Don't forget the meat. Prosciutto and the more evil kinds of salami go well.

As for canned goods, smoked oysters are good; mussels and clams are available in a variety of sauces, and so are sardines. Pickled vegetables such as okra and miniature cobs of corn are a nice addition. To improve upon jumbo stuffed olives, wrap with half-strips of bacon, secure with toothpicks and broil five minutes at 500 degrees.

Keep scrambled eggs warm in a chafing dish. Or, serve slices of hard-cooked egg that have been pickled in vinegar. Have available plenty of cold beer.

64   Complete the meal with a bowl of mixed grapefruit and orange

segments, served tart and icy. It will cut the preceding heavy flavors and cleanse the palate.

The manner of serving this brunch is important. Done carelessly, the buffet will turn into an unappetizing melange. There is nothing wrong with bringing an opened tin of fish to table. In fact, the hash resulting from an effort to transplant sardines from can to plate would be far more offensive than a commercial container. Solve the problem by arranging the tins on a tray. And don't forget separate serving instruments.

65

8

You Can't Go It Alone

Some menus that *require* two in the kitchen

SO YOU LIKE TO COOK. That doesn't necessarily mean that you relish the prospect of a weekend with cleaver and chopping block or paring knife and mounds of vegetables. But some dishes both require and reward that kind of painstaking preparation. The secret is to work together to win the rewards without spending the hours.

Here are two menus, one a lusty chili supper and the other a deceptively simple spring luncheon, that demand ample attention to the blade and the block. Only the most intrepid knife wielder would attempt either by himself, because of wrist fatigue in the first instance and lack of time in the second. Even with two in the kitchen, allow at least a third more time for ingredient preparation than you would initially estimate. Otherwise you may find yourself in the plight of one overly optimistic cook who found herself still cleaning scallions in her dressing gown twenty minutes before the guests were to arrive.

The supper menu features chili as served in West Texas. (Don't
66 get into arguments with self-proclaimed chili purists. The number of

people these days who insist that they know the only way to make chili con carne is almost as large as the number of martini experts fifteen years ago.) This version does not contain beans (serve them on the side), tomatoes (have ketchup handy if you must), flour or ground meat. The proportions for six hearty appetites are:

West Texas Chili

½ pound good suet, preferably kidney fat, well picked over and ground

3 pounds chuck beef or stew beef cut in ½-inch or smaller cubes

2 large or 3 medium onions, chopped—about 3 cups

4 or 5 cloves garlic, minced

3 tablespoons chili powder, or to taste

1 tablespoon salt, or less, to taste

Dried oregano, ground cumin, red pepper flakes as needed (see below)

Beef stock, about 2 cups

Render two or three tablespoons of the suet in a heavy soup pot or Dutch oven. Cook the onions and garlic in the suet until wilted, then remove and reserve. Brown the beef, adding more suet if needed. Stirring, render the remaining suet, then add just enough stock to cover the beef.

Return the onions and garlic to the pot; add chili powder and 2 teaspoons of salt. If your chili powder is light on oregano and cumin flavors, add perhaps a half-teaspoon of oregano and a little less cumin, and if light on heat (many of the best chili powders are), add a half teaspoon of red pepper flakes. If you're not sure, omit the additions for now.

Bring to a boil, then lower heat, cover and simmer for 2½ hours. Taste and correct chili powder, pepper, salt, oregano and cumin. Simmer at least another half hour.

The meat should release enough of its juices that you need not 67

add more stock, but if the meat appears above the surface, add enough liquid to cover. Stir occasionally, not frequently.

You can serve the chili now. It improves, however, if cooled, refrigerated a day or longer and reheated. If you're squeamish about the grease, you can break it off the top of the refrigerated chili and discard most of it before reheating.

With the chili, serve a celery salad (page 82) and crisp-fried tortillas, accompanied by a fiery and flavorful sauce called *salsa cruda*.

Salsa cruda appears at three meals a day as a supplement to salt and pepper on many Mexican tables. Those unaccustomed to strong seasonings are sometimes warned to approach it with caution. Despite its reputation, it need be only as hot as you make it.

The sauce will be more authentic if you use ripe red tomatoes, peeled and seeded, and employ patience, a sharp knife and the help of your cooking partner to chop everything very fine by hand. A grinder, however, makes a short cut possible. This recipe, which includes possible variations, approximates one published by Elena Zelayeta, but we've modified it to suit our tastes.

Salsa Cruda

Chop, grind or blend together the following:

3 large or 4 medium tomatoes, preferably peeled (page 82); you may use green tomatoes for variety

1 bunch scallions with tops

1 sweet pepper (bell or Cuban), split, ribbed and seeded

Hot peppers (see below)

Add the following:

1 teaspoon salt

1 tablespoon wine vinegar

1 tablespoon olive or corn oil (if hot peppers are canned in oil, use that oil instead)

Add *one* of the following herb flavors:

2 tablespoons or more finely chopped cilantro (available at

Chinese, Mexican or Italian food shops; also known as Chinese parsley or coriander), *or*

1 teaspoon dried oregano, rubbed between the palms, *or*

2 tablespoons water, first brought to a boil and then poured over
   1 teaspoon cracked coriander seeds to stand 5 minutes, after which seeds are strained out.

About the hot peppers: preferably handle them with rubber gloves; wash hands and keep hands away from eyes after handling chilis. You should remove the seeds and ribs from most hot peppers, although you can use four "finger peppers" with stem ends removed and seeds included. Seeds make the sauce all the hotter. If you choose dried hot red peppers, soak them in warm water and rib and seed them before chopping. With some exceptions, hot green peppers tend to be hotter than red. One 2-inch by 3-inch hot green chili will make a piquant sauce in this recipe; two or three slender chilis will do as well. For a mild sauce, use a small tin of peeled green chilis. Experiment both as to type and quantity of peppers until you suit your own taste.

The sauce will keep in a tightly covered jar in the refrigerator for several weeks.

Here is a springtime luncheon menu guaranteed to leave every saucepan in your kitchen dirty and every guest in your dining room delighted.

Begin with vichyssoise made the day before, but finished with cream and topped with chopped chives near serving time. Follow with lamb chops and six vegetables. Conclude with Brie and French bread. The best vichyssoise recipe we know is Craig Claiborne's:

Vichyssoise à la Ritz

4 leeks, white part, sliced

1 medium onion, sliced

¼ cup sweet butter

5 medium potatoes, thinly sliced

1 quart chicken broth

1 tablespoon or less salt

3 cups milk

2 cups heavy cream

Chopped chives

In a deep kettle, brown the leeks and onion very lightly in the butter. Add the potatoes, broth and salt, and boil 35 minutes, or until very tender. Crush and rub through a fine sieve or puree in an electric blender.

Return the sieved mixture to the kettle, add the milk and one cup of the cream and bring to a boil. Cool and rub again through a fine sieve. Chill. *(Though Claiborne doesn't say so, at this point we frequently chill it overnight.)* Add the remaining cream. Chill thoroughly and serve garnished with chives.

Lamb Chops and Six (or More) Vegetables

The lamb chops are the easy part. Select the thickest loin cuts you can afford and serve one or two per person, depending on size. Rub with halved garlic, salt and pepper, and broil 15 minutes for medium, turning once. (If, however, you are going to keep them in a warm oven during vegetable preparation and soup eating, cut cooking time to 12 minutes.)

The chop-vegetable combination should appeal as much to the eye as to the palate. On individual plates, surround the chops with small mounds of vegetables. The idea is to provide a tasty mouthful of each, not to fulfill dietary requirements for the week. Insofar as possible, use fresh vegetables and build your selection around those available, with frozen vegetables a distant second choice. Seek variety in color and texture.

The secret to serving gracefully six vegetables in one meal lies in *preparation* and *planning*.

70   **Preparation**—Be particularly careful to arrange the table setting

exactly as you want it before guests arrive. You won't have time later to scramble after the missing salt and pepper or the misplaced cheese plates.

Prepare vegetables for cooking. Wrap in moist paper toweling covered with foil, or preserve under cool water, as for potatoes. Butter sauces should be prepared and kept in melting pots. Place dry herbs in individual wax-paper twists. Start heating a large teakettle of water; having boiling water available is much easier than waiting for the proverbial watched pot. Get out your saucepans and decide what you want to cook in which (and, if you're short of them, which ones can be quickly washed and recycled for the last, shortest-cooking items).

Planning—While two can help with vegetable preparation, the actual cooking should be handled by one. The other partner should confine himself to grilling the chops, which are notorious for fat flare-ups and need close attention. The vegetable chef should make a simple schedule of cooking times, beginning with the vegetable that takes the longest. Make liberal use of the kitchen timer. Since you probably will have more vegetables than surface burners, the early cookers can be warmed briefly after the chops have been removed from the broiler. Sauces can be rewarmed at the last moment with the vegetables they accompany.

By the time you've done all of this, you're ready for a drink. One of the best things about the two-in-the-kitchen routine is that you can serve a delightfully involved meal without deserting your guests beforehand. We usually figure on a short pre-meal period, about half an hour, with this menu, reserving the main conversation time for the table and for coffee and brandy later. During the pre-meal time while the vegetables and chops are cooking, one of the hosts is always available to chat with guests. (Sometimes both make it at once for a minute or two.)

Here's a possible vegetable menu with suggested seasonings and   71 cooking times for fresh vegetables. In all cases, taste to check salt before serving.

1) New potatoes with dill butter: 25-30 minutes. Peel; add one inch boiling salted water; cover and cook, shaking the pan several times. Add finely chopped dill fern to the butter, 1½ teaspoons per four potatoes if fresh or ½ teaspoon if dried. Serve one potato or two very small ones per person.

2) Asparagus with Parmesan: 15 minutes, approximately, depending on size. (Two stalks per person for this menu; more if fewer vegetables are used.) Wash thoroughly, both immersing in water and then spraying to remove grit. Peel the stalks a few inches from the bottom. Either tie stalks and stand them upright in the bottom of a double boiler, covering with the inverted top pan, or lay flat in a covered skillet. Add 2 inches of boiling, salted water to the double boiler or ⅜ inch to the skillet. Simmer for 12 minutes and test for tenderness. Sprinkle with grated cheese (about half a teaspoon per stalk); melted butter optional.

3) Carrots with honey: 7 to 10 minutes to boil, 3 minutes to glaze. Peel and cut in thin rounds. Cook in small amount of boiling water. Drain. Place in skillet or heavy saucepan with just enough honey to coat the bottom. Heat with flame on low, turning frequently until lightly browned.

4) Peas with mint: 8 to 10 minutes. Shell; cook in a small amount of boiling salted water, reducing to simmer. Dress with butter to which chopped mint leaves, either fresh or dried, have been added.

5) Spinach with crumbled bacon bits: 3 to 5 minutes, if you prepare the bacon ahead of time. One bacon slice for each two servings should suffice. Follow for spinach the previous directions for washing asparagus. Wet leaves heavily before placing in pan; no additional water is needed. Steam at low heat in a tightly covered pan, shaking occasionally. Add a shake or two of red wine vinegar and the crumbled bacon.

72   6) Tomatoes with basil or oregano: 2 minutes. Dot tomato halves

Asparagus: Tie stalks in a bundle and stand up in 2 inches of water in the bottom of a double boiler, over which the top will be inverted.

with butter ahead of time; add salt and sprinkle with ¼ teaspoon of chosen herb per serving. Run under the broiler after taking out the chops.

Once all six vegetables are under way, it's time to serve the soup. The chops (a little underdone and wrapped in foil to prevent drying) can be kept warm in the oven and the vegetables quickly heated. After soup, while one cook serves the chops and vegetables, the other readies the cheese plates.

Try to do all this by yourself, however, and you'd be ready for the funny farm.

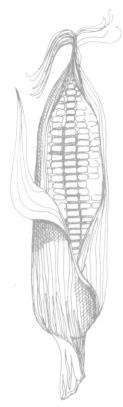

The Unexpected Vegetable

Cooked or raw, vice versa's a virtue

FOR AT LEAST 25 centuries, the Chinese have been careful not to overcook vegetables. In the last 50 years many Americans have learned the same lesson. Oddly though, perhaps for sanitary reasons, the Chinese serve few vegetables raw, and they cook, ever so lightly, a number of things like lettuce, watercress and cucumbers.

The authors have acquired a name for originality in serving vegetables by the rule, "Vice versa's a vegetable virtue." Here are some ideas (French, Italian, Chinese and native American) for serving raw some things your guests expect to see cooked, serving cooked some things they expect to see raw, and making them like it.

Les Crudités

Crisp, cool vegetables and a hot dip make a cocktail relish or an appetizer that will please in any kind of weather. Use the following unexpected raw vegetables: broccoli flowerets, cauliflower flowerets, asparagus tips, thin slices of turnip (yes, raw!), zucchini slices and 75 mushrooms. Add the standard raw relishes —celery (leaves remaining), white or red radishes, scallions. Cleaning and preparing *les crudités* takes time, and you'll be grateful to have two cooks at two chopping blocks.

Make *bagna cauda* ("hot bath") to go with them. Mix together:

1 pint olive oil
4 cloves garlic, finely chopped
8 anchovy fillets, very finely chopped
½ teaspoon oregano
Salt and pepper

Heat slowly over low heat, not letting the garlic brown, but mashing the anchovy bits into the oil so that they almost disintegrate. Serve over low flame in chafing dish.

Zucchini Canapes

Zucchini appetizers are easier. Remove the fuzz but not the skin from tender young zucchini, using plastic scrubber and being careful not to bruise. Cut thin slices and spread with a sharp cheese spread. Cold, leftover Welsh rabbit (page 123) is ideal. Sprinkle lightly with paprika and pass with drinks.

Not being sailors, we've never tried it, but we admire the thought suggested by Barbara Rosenfeld and Ellen Kurzman several years ago in a *Potomac* magazine article entitled "Cooking on a Boat." It is based on the fact that freezing some vegetables breaks down their fibers in somewhat the same way that preliminary cooking would; this is why cooking times can be shorter for frozen than for fresh vegetables. Rosenfeld and Kurzman therefore suggest using frozen green peas to help keep other foods cold in the early stages of a cruise; then, when the peas thaw, using them uncooked for a salad.

For a different way of cooking such green vegetables as spinach or broccoli, try the Chinese method given on page 91, or stuff a cucumber Chinese-style:

Stuffed Cucumbers

2 medium cucumbers, peeled, cut crosswise into 4 or 5 segments
    and seeded

¼ pound ground pork

½ to 1 teaspoon minced ginger root

1 tablespoon sherry (a substitute for rice wine)

1 tablespoon soy sauce

1 teaspoon salt

1 teaspoon sugar (*not*, in this case, optional)

¼ teaspoon MSG

Peanut oil

Mix the pork, ginger, sherry, soy sauce, half the salt and the sugar. Stuff into cucumber sections. Heat a heavy skillet over high heat and add only enough oil to cover the bottom. Brown each end of the cucumber sections for about 2 minutes. Add ¼ cup cold water, bring to a boil, cover and reduce heat to moderate. Cook two minutes, then add the MSG and remaining salt. Cover and cook 15 minutes more. Serve as a side dish for four in a Chinese or Western meal.

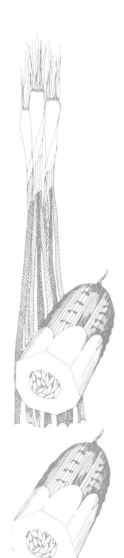

Braised Lettuce or Endive

Or cook your salad greens as a side dish for meat or fish, accompanied by one of the "Salads without Greens" of the next chapter. Braised greens have an unexpected flavor too little known in American homes.

Use by choice Boston or bibb lettuce, although romaine or escarole also may be cooked, if the tough outer leaves are removed. Iceberg has more taste this way than when used in salad; Boston lettuce not only retains its taste but takes on a less offensive texture.

Greens for 4 servings (2 Boston or 4 bibb heads, or ½ large head
    of iceberg)

4 tablespoons butter

¾ cup chicken stock

Salt and pepper

Halve Boston; leave bibb heads whole; break heads of larger varieties into four pieces. Wash thoroughly, spreading leaves slightly apart and removing those that are crushed or bruised. Dry thoroughly on paper towels.

Melt butter in a large skillet; saute greens quickly, slightly browning the outer leaves. Add the stock, cover and simmer just until the leaves are wilted and tender. The greens will have a pleasant if hay-like flavor that goes particularly well with broiled fish.

(When using escarole in a normal raw salad, tear off and save the tough outer leaves; cook them Chinese style, as you would spinach, for a next-day meal.)

Endive also can be braised. It takes on a zestiness quite appropriate to steak or game. Use one head of Belgian endive per person, brown on all sides and if you wish, use beef broth or consomme rather than chicken stock.

Wilted Lettuce

Wilted lettuce takes your greens back to the salad bowl, but cooks them ever so slightly in a hot dressing. Use any kind of lettuce, but do not mix firm with tender varieties; the cooking times would clash. Endive and watercress are not recommended for this treatment. Spinach is, and tender dandelion greens, though a nuisance to clean and rib, respond well with the addition of the least suspicion of sugar.

Greens for 4 servings (see above recipe)

6 slices bacon

⅓ cup mild vinegar

2 tablespoons chopped green onions, including some of the green tops

Salt and pepper

78   Cut the bacon into squares and fry crisp, pouring off and reserv-

ing the fat as it accumulates. Drain bacon on absorbent paper and return fat to skillet. Saute onion until slightly wilted. Add vinegar and bring to a boil. Add greens and toss quickly until just wilted. Add salt and freshly ground pepper to taste. Serve topped with the crisp bacon squares.

That's vegetables vice versa: eat asparagus raw; cook lettuce. If you're not confused yet, then try "Salads Without Greens."

79

Salads Without Greens

No fruits need apply

YOU'RE PLANNING Sunday meals; the menu demands a salad, and the corner grocery, the only available source of food supply that day, doesn't carry greens. To complete the picture, the notion of combining a limp canned peach half, a scoop of cottage cheese and a maraschino cherry and calling it a salad turns you off.

Preserving salad greens for any length of time is a tricky business at best. Romaine and iceberg lettuce outlast other varieties. But they offer an extremely limited ingredient list for a mixed green salad, and some say that iceberg is fit only for pet rabbits and tortoises anyway.

If you are bent on a green salad, here are some ways to help preserve greens from your Saturday morning marketing until Sunday dinner. Put the bunch of watercress in a glass of cold water, cover the top with plastic wrap, anchor with a rubber band and refrigerate. Wash leaf lettuce, but do not separate leaves. Allow some moisture to remain, encase in a plastic bag and refrigerate. If you have a large quantity of greens, use a moistened pillow case; it will work better than a plastic bag.

For those who don't want to take a chance on wilted lettuce, here are some salads without greens.

Green and Gold Salad

10-ounce package fresh spinach (try to get tender young leaves)
2 medium carrots (approximately)

Dressing:

3 tablespoons olive oil
2 tablespoons peanut or corn oil
2 tablespoons lemon juice
¼ teaspoon dry mustard

Mix the oils, juice and seasonings. Wash spinach, remove stems and drain on towel. After peeling and trimming the carrots, use the same swivel-bladed knife with which you peeled them to make long carrot curls. The proportion of spinach to carrot most attractive to the eye also tastes best. Toss well with the dressing, just enough to coat. If desired, garnish with chopped egg yolk.

Farmer Salad

This salad resembles one served at the late Goldie Ahearn's restaurant in Washington and makes a vegetarian lunch all by itself. Or in small servings, it is an excellent accompaniment to chops.

In individual salad bowls or soup plates, place a thin layer of bite-size pieces of leaf lettuce or romaine. Atop this, arrange the following fresh, uncooked vegetables (plus any others that suit your fancy): asparagus tips, cauliflower flowerets, scallions (including green tops), thick unpeeled (⅜ inch) slices of cucumber, halved or quartered red radishes. Serve with a bowl of well-salted sour cream or your favorite Roquefort or other blue cheese dressing. Let the diner sauce his own salad.

Salade à la Russe

To prepare this vegetable melange at painstaking best, numerous kinds of vegetables should be cooked individually, cooled, diced and   81 marinated in sauce vinaigrette, and bound with mayonnaise.

Our shortcut proposes a temporary alliance between Russia and Greece: mixed vegetables *a là Grècque*. Buy the finest frozen mixed vegetables you can find, with a minimum of carrot and potato content. For each 10-ounce package, make a cooking liquid in the following proportions:

½ cup water

¼ cup olive oil

1 clove garlic, crushed in press

Juice of one lemon

Sprig of parsley

1 bay leaf

4 peppercorns

Tie the last three ingredients in a wisp of cheesecloth for easy removal. Cook the minimum cooking time stated on the vegetable package, then chill in the cooking liquid. When quite cold, drain and bind with a minimum of mayonnaise, about 2 tablespoons. If desired, small cubes of cheddar or crumbled bacon bits may be added at the last minute. Serve mounded over a thin bed of lettuce (if you have it).

Celery Salad (with Curry)

To serve four, combine six ribs of celery, sliced in very thin rounds and including leaves, with 3 tablespoons olive oil, 1 tablespoon lemon juice, ¾ teaspoon salt, ¼ teaspoon dry mustard and ½ teaspoon curry powder. Toss and allow to age at room temperature for at least one hour, but not more than an hour and a half.

Tomatoes with Basil

This salad is the simplest of all. Select tomatoes that are ripe and ready. Plunge into boiling water for 30 seconds, then into ice water. This procedure loosens the skin for peeling. Peel and slice into thin rounds. For two tomatoes, mix 1 tablespoon olive oil, 1 teaspoon

wine vinegar, ½ teaspoon dried basil, ¼ teaspoon dry mustard, ¼ teaspoon salt and six grinds of the peppermill. Sprinkle the seasoning over the tomatoes and serve at room temperature.

The tomatoes will taste even better if you can obtain fresh basil, but use four times the dried amount—2 teaspoons, finely chopped.

Cucumbers and Yogurt

Peel, slice and arrange the cucumbers on a plate. Spread with a thin layer of plain yogurt. Add ¼ teaspoon per person of crushed dried mint (better still, 1 teaspoon per person of finely chopped, fresh mint leaves). Allow to stand one hour before serving.

Stuffed Tomatoes

Parboil the tomatoes: dip them into boiling water for 30 seconds, but don't peel them this time. Drain and cool; cut off a thin slice from the stem end and scoop out center with a melon scoop. Meanwhile cook for five minutes in boiling water about two ears of corn for every three tomatoes. Cool, then scrape off the corn kernels and mix with chopped, sauteed bell pepper (about 3 parts corn to 1 part pepper). Salt well and add a few grinds of black pepper. Stuff the tomatoes with the corn and pepper mixture. (If there's corn left over, you can use it in a mixed salad the next day.) Before serving at room temperature, sprinkle with crisp bacon bits.

Green Beans (with Help)

Don't bother with this recipe unless you have fresh beans. Wash and cut into ½-inch lengths. Have boiling water ready in kettle. Salt beans lightly and place in saucepan. Barely cover with boiling water. Place lid on pan and simmer about ten minutes, testing for tenderness after eight. Drain and chill. Mix with 1 tablespoon per serving of finely chopped purple onion. Apply a vinegar and oil dressing, and allow to stand one hour in the refrigerator before serving.

Would You Believe Mushrooms and Asparagus?

This salad is glorious for spring. In many parts of the country, a two-week period in the spring turns into Camelot for asparagus lovers. 83

The spears are thin and new green; the true fan doesn't mind eating the vegetable every day in one guise or another. Simmer the spears in a modicum of boiling salted water until just tender. A skillet will do this nicely. Test after six minutes. Drain and cool. Have ready small, white, firm fresh mushroom caps from which you have pulled the stems. Combine gently with the asparagus spears; dress with three parts oil, one part vinegar and salt and pepper to taste. Marinate one hour.

A final note on cleaning vegetables: If *cooked* spinach, asparagus or other vegetables have to be clean, the raw or parboiled variety has to be even cleaner. Spinach should be totally immersed three or four times and carefully spot checked for sand. Asparagus tips must be gently worked with the fingers under a hard stream of cool water. Easily bruised vegetables should be rubbed gently with a plastic scrub brush.

The Hyphenated-American Menu

**Making a hit with ethnic
specialties in a nonethnic meal**

THERE ARE state dinners for twenty to a thousand, family-reunion dinners for a dozen or more, dinners to pay social debts for eight to twenty. All of these occasions are necessary and can be accomplished successfully.

Nonetheless, time and custom have established that the ideal number of people at table is either two or six. (M.F.K. Fisher says *one,* two or six; she argues the point so well that to review her argument would be presumptuous.)

With the equipment and space of the average small kitchen of the average small family without servants, it *is* possible to prepare for six a classic French dinner. But without the equipment and manpower of either a professional kitchen or that of a rich man, your menu planning should be limited to no more than one of the elegant dishes that may include three or more involved, freshly made sauces. Other dishes must be simpler.

To prepare a complete Chinese or Japanese meal for more than four requires more space and equipment than the small kitchen likely   85 affords. Even if it were feasible, the meal would suffer from lack of variety. Chinese dishes, particularly either the red-cooked or the stir-fried, do not easily multiply or divide; too much or too little food in a single *wok* invites disaster. And the standard rule calls for one dish per person up to about eight or twelve persons, all dishes to be shared equally. Beyond twelve, one makes two recipes of several dishes—but each doubled recipe needs two *woks!*

Thus an authentic national menu for the ideal six is unlikely without expenditure of an unlikely amount of time, money and storage plans for equipment. (Mexican and Hungarian menus are, for the most part, happy exceptions.)

The four so-called classic cuisines are French, Chinese, Italian and German (and many would omit the last). Most widely honored, of course, is the French. Yet it is not unknown in the French cuisine to include a dish such as *asperges chinoises*. We discussed Chinese asparagus in Chapter I, where we found the authentic Chinese (or French) version inferior to Asparagus East, the Chinese-derived American version. You may see on menus *crevettes a l'indienne,* a delicious but modified and not very Indian (*or* British) version of curried shrimp. The pressed duck for which the French are justly famous has a much more Chinese than French approach to the palate.

The French have not been above borrowing ideas and dishes from other cuisines. There is reason to believe that the Chinese, via Marco Polo, inspired much that is great about Italian cooking, and not merely pasta. There is incontrovertible evidence that the birth of what we know as French cuisine was attended by Italian chefs as midwives. One of us would choose northern Italian cooking, the other the northern version of Chinese, over all but the most exquisite of classic French cooking.

Face the fact that one rarely, except through expending much money, sits down to a classic French meal. More likely, even in our own favorite French restaurants, the menu is a *mélange* of a few classic French dishes filled out with peasant French items or the ubiquitous "continental" fare. Because "continental" really means "hotel international," the menu may well include American or British or Hungarian or Greek standbys.

So what's wrong, given these examples, with crossing the border on your menu? Though we have prepared dinners in which every dish was Japanese or Mexican and served them to six or more from a small kitchen without a servant, the equipment and space strain made these dinners less than enjoyable evenings for the hosts. A little thought about tastes, leading to imaginative menu planning, will enable you to incorporate two or more national cuisines, with their distinctive taste attitudes, into a single successful meal.

Scattered through this book (and indexed separately by national origin) are recipes from the French, Chinese, Italian, British, Spanish, Mexican and Hungarian cuisines, as well as native American or "continental" dishes. They all should, with one exception, fit some international menu. The exception, West Texas chili, is more Texan than Mexican (as American as chop suey and pizza) and thus can fit as a Mexican motif in casual American menus.

This chapter offers three of the most versatile recipes that we know for international menu planning. Two are Chinese, one Japanese. Though two require special ingredients, none requires special equipment.

China: Szechuan Duck

It has been noted (M.F.K. Fisher again) that the world's first great cookbook was published about the 27th century B.C. Master K'ung, known in the West as Confucius, further codified the techniques of Chinese cooking in the 5th century B.C. This is old stuff.

Rice, including fried rice, is discussed in the next chapter, and cooked cucumbers are also in our Chinese repertoire. But as an example of an international dish which can fit an international menu, you must consider Szechuan duck. Love if you will (many gourmands do) the orange and cherry flavors the French give duck. But as rebels against almost all sweet meats, we respectfully refer you to the Chinese as the supreme masters of this bird.

Each region of China has its own particular version of duck; in our opinion, that classic one called Peking duck is not for the home kitchen. Craig Claiborne has published a viable technique for making Peking duck at home, but we feel the same way about preparation of Peking duck as Escoffier does about turtle soup; unless you absolutely have to, don't make it at home; instead buy it from an expert.

Buying from specialists is the ordinary practice of the food-proud Cantonese; their province's version of duck can be found hanging for sale, whole or by the piece, in food stores and what we would call delicatessens throughout the Chinatowns of America.

Newly popular in the United States is the food of Szechuan province. Tongue-broiling quantities of pepper characterize many dishes, though not the one given here.

Szechuan duck can well be prepared at home. The few unusual ingredients it contains can be purchased in Chinese or international stores or by mail order, and the equipment it requires is found in almost every American kitchen. This duck's versatility in menu-planning should become legendary. It can substitute for the goose at a buffet breakfast, the turkey for a small family's holiday meal, or the broiled chicken for a festive luncheon.

The duck is by stages washed, seasoned, steamed, dried, fried and carved in its special way; thus it takes time—at least 13 or 14 hours. Start in the early, early morning, or the day before. Not one of the stages is beyond the capability of a careful beginning cook. Obviously the second person in the kitchen will wind up doing most of the rest of the meal.

The recipe:

1 Long Island duck, about 5 pounds
2 tablespoons salt
1 tablespoon Szechuan peppercorns, crushed with rolling pin or

chopped 3 seconds in blender at high speed. (Ordinary peppercorns are a different spice entirely and will not do.)
3 scallions, including green tops, cut in 2-inch pieces and crushed lightly with flat of knife
4 slices (about ¼ inch thick) fresh ginger, scrubbed but unpeeled
2 tablespoons soy sauce—preferably Chinese, such as Amoy. (Japanese, such as Kikkoman, is a poor substitute; American soy sauce doesn't have the correct flavor for this dish.)
1 teaspoon Chinese five-spices powder (optional)
3 cups peanut oil

Thaw the duck thoroughly if frozen, reserving neck and giblets for duck soup. (The backbone will join them after the duck is cooked, and we also like, in a most un-Chinese way, to cut off the wings and save them for soup.) Wash and dry the duck thoroughly, inside and out.

Mix the salt, Szechuan peppercorns, scallion pieces and ginger slices. Take part of this mixture and rub thoroughly inside the duck, leaving at least a piece of ginger and two pieces of scallion in the cavity. Place the duck on its back and, with the flat of the hands, crush the rib cage, flattening the duck. (The bones are more brittle than those of a chicken and are easily crushed.) Now rub the outside of the duck, pressing the remainder of the ginger and scallion mixture firmly into the skin. If you have removed the wings, fasten the neck skin loosely over the exposed meat with toothpicks. Refrigerate the duck for six hours or overnight.

If you have a Chinese or other steamer in which the duck can be steamed without the water touching it, use it. Otherwise, improvise a steamer. Take a roasting pan with a flat bottom rack. Either use a vegetable steaming rack in the empty pan or balance the flat bottom rack on several shallow empty food cans with both ends cut out. Pour in sufficient water to come within an inch of the rack. Bring to a boil on top of the stove. Meanwhile, mix the soy sauce and, optionally, five-spices powder and rub the duck inside and out, letting some of the 89 liquid remain in the cavity. Put the duck, breast up, on a heat-proof plate and place it on the rack in your steamer (not touching the sides). Cover (with the vents, if any, closed) and steam on top of the stove for two hours. Keep a kettle of water boiling to replenish the liquid as needed, taking care not to pour water over duck. After steaming, let the duck rest for half an hour, lid still on.

The duck is now so tender that it must be handled with care to prevent it from falling apart. Using heat-proof mitts, invert another plate over the duck. Holding the bird firmly between the plates, turn quickly so that the duck rests breast down. Return what is now the bottom plate and the duck to the steamer; cover and let rest without new heat for another half hour.

Gently brush off the scallion and ginger pieces and discard. Rest the duck, back down, on a plate covered with several thicknesses of absorbent paper. Let cool and dry in front of an electric fan or in a breezy corner for three or more hours. (Refrigeration at this point would tend to make the duck less crisp after it is fried.)

Heat the three cups of oil to 380 degrees in a *wok* (round-bottomed Chinese frying vessel) or a large skillet. An electric skillet makes temperature control easier. Moving the duck carefully with two large pancake turners, lower the duck, back down, into the oil and fry at 380 degrees for 15 minutes. Move the duck slightly two or three times to prevent sticking.

Carefully lift the duck back onto a plate, invert another plate over it, and flip onto the breast side. (If you try to turn the duck using the turners alone, you may break a leg—your own if you spill grease on the floor, but more likely the duck's.) Then using the two turners, return the duck to the oil and fry breast side down a final 15 minutes, The skin should now be quite crisp and a somewhat deeper than golden brown.

To carve, cut off the legs (and wings, if you did not remove them before). Using *choy doh,* heavy French knife or poultry shears, cut the duck in half lengthwise and remove the backbone entirely (reserve for soup). Then cut crosswise every 1 to 1½ inches so as to leave the carcass in 10 to 12 pieces (five or six from each side). Arrange them on a platter, breast side up, so as to reconstruct the duck. Put legs and, optionally, wings back in place. Garnish with shredded lettuce and serve.

The Chinese eat this dish, bones and all, in little sandwiches made with steamed buns. The buns do not agree with many Western tastes, nor do the bones. But a push of fork or chopstick removes the tender meat and crisp skin.

The duck soup for which you've reserved bony parts and giblets has only accidental Chinese overtones, so we write of it elsewhere (p. 000). But before leaving China, learn a way of cooking vegetables which can embellish a meal from any cuisine and does not taste distinctively Chinese; just distinctively good.

China: Vegetables

10-ounce package washed spinach
2 tablespoons peanut oil
1 clove garlic
1 teaspoon salt
½ teaspoon sugar (optional)
Pinch of MSG (optional)

Peel the garlic and crush under flat of a knife (a *choy doh* does it most easily). Heat the oil and garlic in a saucepan over high heat. Add the spinach and stir thoroughly to coat with oil. Discard garlic, add salt and optional ingredients; stir, cover and cook for 1½-2 minutes. Serve immediately.

The same method works equally well for celery, cabbage or *bok choy*, and we've read it recommended for watercress. It can be adapted for firmer green vegetables such as broccoli by (1) parboiling for five minutes the cleaned, cut broccoli before adding to the oil; (2) adding half a cup of water before covering the pan, and (3) cooking appropriately longer—say 5 minutes instead of 2—after covering. 91

Japan: Suimono

This classic clear soup, beautiful both in taste and appearance, not only fits well into many Western menus but also offers the opportunity to use successfully a "convenience food." The base of the soup is *dashi,* made from dried bonito flakes and dried seaweed (properly kelp). Japanese cooks make *ichiban* (first) *dashi;* then, with the used bonito flakes and a smaller portion of new ones, *niban* (second) *dashi* for use as a cooking stock.

Forget it. Buy *dashi-no-moto,* best described as "soup bags" by analogy with tea bags. Place one bag in three cups of water and boil gently for 10 minutes. Remove the bag and you have *dashi.*

Add from ½ teaspoon to 2 teaspoons Japanese soy sauce. You must experiment, starting with the smallest amount, to determine how much you want. Add salt to taste, and now you have *suimono.*

But *suimono* is lost without its garnishes. Into each of four soup plates, place a center slice from a fresh mushroom, a sliver of lemon peel, a small leaf of steamed spinach, a lightly cooked curl of carrot and, if you can get it, a thin slice or two of Japanese fish cake (*kamaboko*). Pour soup over it all and serve with almost any menu.

To most palates, it doesn't even taste fishy.

12

Five Kinds of Rice

And a passing bow to barley

THOUGH WE URGE mixing in one menu dishes of different national origin, it would be rather silly to serve an Italian meat dish with Japanese style rice. Rice is a mainstay of the Anderson style of cooking, and it's far from infrequent that one of us, tied up with a main course, will ask the other, "Will you do the rice?" Often as we've done it, we don't always remember immediately the proportions for the particular method needed for the meal at hand. Therefore, this chapter collects in one place the five ways of cooking rice we use most often so that *we* can find them more readily; we hope it will be as useful to you.

Then we'll examine a couple of other grains and some variations which may give you courage in international experimentation. For example, we take barley, a grain most often associated with Scotland, and treat it in the way the Mexicans and Chinese treat rice.

All recipes serve four.   93

Chinese Rice

Wash one cup of long-grain rice in a sieve until the water runs clear, then add it to 1¾ cups cold cooking water, in a 3-quart saucepan. Bring to a boil over high heat, then cover and cook over low heat for 20 to 25 minutes. The liquid will have disappeared and small holes will appear on the surface of the rice. Leave covered and standing, but off the heat, for another 25 minutes. Stir well with a fork or chopsticks and serve. Or, if desired for fried rice, thoroughly refrigerate before frying.

Japanese Rice

For each cup of thoroughly washed long-grain rice, use 1¼ cups cold water in a 2-quart saucepan (larger, of course, if you multiply the recipe). Cook, covered, over low heat for 25 minutes. Let rest 5 minutes, then stir and serve.

Indian Rice

This method works very well for most American menus, as well as for curry feasts.

Into at least two quarts of boiling, well-salted (2 tablespoons) water, drop one cup of well-washed long-grain rice. Boil exactly 13 minutes and at the same time bring a tea kettle of water to boiling.

Pour the rice into a sieve or fine colander, then blanch it with cold tapwater. Reheat the rice by pouring the kettle of boiling water over it; you may also place the colander of rice over a pan of lightly boiling water, covering the colander with a clean towel while the steam heats the rice.

Italian Rice

If you can, use imported Italian rice for this basic risotto; if not, use well-washed long-grain rice.

1 cup rice

1 small onion, minced (⅜ to ½ cup)

1½ tablespoons butter

2 cups chicken broth, approximately

Pinch of saffron (less than ⅛ teaspoon)

Heat oven to 375 degrees. In a skillet, melt the butter over medium heat and cook the onion until transparent. Add the rice and stir until well coated with butter and heated through but *not* (according to a northern Italian grandmother) browned.

Transfer the contents of the skillet to a one-quart casserole. Add the meager but essential saffron and barely cover the rice with boiling chicken broth. Stir. Cover and place in the oven for 45 minutes, stirring after 25 minutes. If a moister rice is desired, add the remaining chicken broth when you stir at the 25-minute mark. Taste for seasoning then, because depending upon the chicken broth, you may want to add salt. If a drier rice is desired, remove the cover five minutes before the rice is done.

Wild Rice

This is not truly rice, but it is truly as delicious as it is expensive. A pound of it lasts us almost a year, so infrequently do we use it, but no grain we know cooks up in quite such luxurious form. Of all the various cooking methods, this one is perhaps the most foolproof, and may be used for any quantity of wild rice.

Place the well-washed rice (one cup for four people) in a small saucepan, cover with cold water and bring to a rolling boil. Remove from heat, cover and let sit for 20 minutes. Drain into a strainer, return rice to the saucepan and repeat the operation. Drain and repeat a third time, this time adding ½ teaspoon salt to the cold water. After the third draining, the rice is ready.

Season with butter or at table with sauce from Steak Diane or, for a festive main-course dish at a light brunch, try . . .

Wild Rice, Mushrooms and Bacon

Crisp four strips of bacon, then saute in the bacon grease the caps from ½ pound of small mushrooms. Mix the mushrooms and bacon grease in the rice (one cup of raw rice cooked as above) and garnish with the bacon.

95

Baked Barley

Barley is worth more than helping fill beer cans and providing limp squiggles in canned soups. Later in the book ▮▮▮▮▮ barley informs one of the simplest of hearty soups; here it appears in its most pristine form:

Preheat oven to 300 degrees. Over 1½ cups pearled barley in a 1-quart casserole, pour 1 cup of boiling chicken broth. Cover and bake for 45 minutes. Add another cup of boiling chicken broth, cover and bake another 30 minutes.

At this point, the barley may be uncovered and returned to the oven for about another 10 minutes, until fairly dry, and served as is. Or it may be used in one of the dishes below.

Barley with Chilis and Cheese

To one recipe of baked barley, add 2 tablespoons soft butter, a 4-ounce can of chopped green chilis (drained), 6 ounces Monterrey Jack cheese cut in small cubes. Stir. Return uncovered to oven for 15 minutes, or until the cheese has melted. Serve.

Barley with Mushrooms

Add to the baked barley ½ cup sliced, lightly sauteed mushrooms and 3 tablespoons grated Parmesan cheese. Bake uncovered for 10 to 25 minutes, until fairly dry, at 350 degrees.

Barley with Almonds

Toss a half cup of slivered almonds in sizzling butter, then add the almonds to the barley. Bake uncovered at 350 degrees for 10 to 15 minutes, or until fairly dry.

All of these baked barley dishes go well with pork or with hearty, unstuffed fowl. Barley with almonds is particularly nice with Cornish hens. Before introducing the most surprising barley dish we know, let's pause for . . .

Fried Rice

1 recipe Chinese rice, thoroughly refrigerated (cook the rice at breakfast time for use at supper, or two or three nights later)

2 eggs

½ cup diced cooked country ham, preferably Smithfield

¼ cup scallions, including green tops, cut in ¼-inch or smaller rings

½ package snow peas, thawed and, if desired, cut in half

2 tablespoons soy sauce, preferably Chinese

½ teaspoon sugar (optional but recommended)

¼ teaspoon MSG

½ cup plus 1 tablespoon peanut oil

Beat eggs and scramble lightly in 1 tablespoon of the oil. Add no seasonings, milk or water. Drain on absorbent paper.

Heat the remaining ½ cup oil in a *wok* or 12-inch cast-iron skillet. When the oil is almost smoking, add the scallions and pea pods and stir a few times.

Add rice. Stir quickly with *wok* shovel (*wok chan*) or pancake turner to coat well with oil, using short chopping strokes to break up any clumps. Add soy sauce, sugar and MSG; stir until rice is the same color throughout. Toss in ham and scrambled eggs. Mix, breaking the eggs into small bits. Serve immediately.

Fried Barley

After the second baking, remove barley from casserole, stir while still warm, refrigerate thoroughly and stir again. Then use it instead of rice in the recipe above. It's Chinese only by inheritance, but it works.

We've even fried wild rice (and used it to stuff parboiled green sweet peppers); its grains are so separate when cooked as suggested earlier that only thorough draining and not refrigeration is required.

Rice with Chinese Sausage

When Chinese rice comes to a boil and you are about to cover it for steaming, place on top a few Chinese pork sausages (*lop chong*).

The sausages will flavor the rice; the dish may either be served immediately or used to make sausage fried rice. (Cut the sausage in slices about ⅜ to ¼-inch thick and substitute ½ cup of it for the ham in the previous fried rice recipe.)

The sausages, cooked over steaming rice this way, may not look done, but they are.

The Well Planned Leftover

**A small family's guide to the Smithfield ham,
and why you should buy a bigger beef
roast than you can possibly eat**

BUYING MORE MEAT than you can eat in a week can make not only
for better cooking but for surprising economy. The secret is to know
when you buy what looks like half a cow just what meals lie in the future. Frequently the later ones are even better than the first. This is
the small family's guide to the Smithfield ham and the standing rib
roast.

Country Ham

Only a large party will demolish a whole Smithfield or other
country (dry) ham. Usually, planning its use begins in the butcher
shop. We choose the largest available Smithfield and ask the butcher
to cut off the hock, which we use later for pea soup.

Then we ask him to cut frying slices beginning with the shank
and continuing right on almost to the biggest part of the butt. Many 99

of these are smaller than center-cut slices, of course, but are large enough for small breakfasts, hot sandwiches and, as the slices get larger, for such a dinner as the southern New Year feast described in the next chapter (page 105). Store the slices in wax-paper bags; they need to be refrigerated but need not be frozen.

This leaves the large end of the ham for boiling and baking, a handy meal for a pre-theater buffet. Your butcher may warn you that the butt end of the ham is hard to carve because of the bones that join there, but he would still charge more for the butt than for the shank if you were to buy only half a ham. That is why we urge you to buy a whole one.

If you have any amateur butcher skills, we recommend you boil the ham, then bone it and roll it before baking. If you are afraid to try this, you can have the ham boned and rolled by the butcher, but cooking it without the bone will sacrifice some of the flavor. If you know your butcher very, very well, perhaps you can boil the ham butt, then take it back to his shop with the stuffing you plan to use and have him bone, stuff and tie it for you.

Use the easy new way of boiling (actually steaming) your country ham. Scrub it with soap and water, rinse well, then let it soak three hours in clear water. Rinse again and place in a covered roasting pan with seven cups of boiling water. Put the ham in an oven which you won't need for any other purpose for at least 10 hours and turn the oven regulator to 500 degrees. Allow your oven the time it needs to reach that temperature (usually 10 to 15 minutes) plus 15 minutes more. Then turn off the heat and let ham coast for three hours. *Do not open the oven door!*

Heat the oven to 500 degrees again—long enough to reach that heat, plus 15 minutes more. Turn off heat. Let ham sit overnight in the still-unopened oven.

Your ham is now what the packing houses call "fully cooked"— but not yet ready to eat. Remove the skin and excess fat. If you're

brave, bone the ham, stuff it if desired, then roll tightly and tie with twine every two inches or so. For stuffing, we use half a cup of ricotta or other small-curd cottage cheese, a teaspoon of dried oregano crushed between the palms, two or three cloves of garlic, slivered, and salt and pepper to taste.

Score the remaining surface fat in one-inch diamonds, placing a whole clove at each intersection. Coat with your favorite ham glaze (we mix brown sugar, dry mustard and sherry; or, more simply, molasses and dry mustard) and bake at 400 degrees for 30 minutes. Serve warm or cold in the thinnest slices you can cut.

Roast Beef

A standing rib roast should be at least three ribs and preferably five, we think, for best cooking. A small family will have more than half the roast left after the first sumptuous dinner with Yorkshire pudding. (See Chapter I, page 19, for roast beef and a Yorkshire pudding recipe.)

There certainly will be sandwiches for school lunches and suppers (enhanced, perhaps, by butter creamed with lemon juice and freshly grated horseradish). But there should also be at least three main meals remaining from a large roast.

The Absolute Hash

Dice a quarter of a pound of bacon, about a cup and a half of cooked beef and two or three small boiled potatoes (about a cup). Cook the bacon until brown but not too crisp, pouring off and reserving the fat.

In about half the fat, wilt ½ cup chopped onion, two or three minced cloves of garlic, ¼ cup chopped green pepper and, if desired, a chopped rib of celery. Now mix together all ingredients, including fat. Add ¼ cup heavy cream.

Cook in a heavy skillet for half an hour over medium heat, shaking or carefully running a spatula under the mixture occasionally to prevent sticking. If you can, flip the hash onto a plate to show the crusty side. If not, simply serve from the skillet.

Beef Mazatlan Style

Dice cooked beef into half-inch pieces; one cupful serves two or three people. Dice the same amount of slightly undercooked boiled potatoes. In a heavy skillet, brown the beef on all sides in a quarter-inch of peanut oil. Remove and keep warm while browning the potato cubes in the same oil.

Have ready shredded lettuce, cooked crisp green beans, lightly fried zucchini slices, sliced ripe raw tomatoes, and wedges of ripe avocado. Cucumbers, sauteed eggplant and other fine things may be added or substituted; ripe olives may be added at the top layer.

In individual soup plates, surround a layer of beef with lettuce. Place potatoes on top, then other vegetables in layers, ending with the raw vegetables. Over all, let each person pour a good hot sauce— a canned taco sauce or homemade *salsa cruda* (page 68), lightly heated.

Devil's Bones

Cut apart the leftover bones from your last week's rib roast. Roll them in lightly beaten egg, then in seasoned bread crumbs. Fry lightly in vegetable oil until crumbs are golden brown on all sides, or broil at low heat.

Top with a canned or homemade *sauce diable;* a fast substitute is to add lemon juice and a strong prepared mustard to heated canned beef gravy. Chopped onion, lightly fried, and chopped capers are optional in the sauce.

Roast Goose

If you choose this wasteful but delicious fowl for a holiday dinner, remember two precautions:

1) Carefully remove all the goose fat as it accumulates in the roaster and save it in a jar. It is a superb cooking fat. Thinly sliced potatoes, fried in it, take on classic proportions.

2) Do not serve champagne with the first meal from the goose. It is the second (and usually final) meal that calls for it: cold goose

sandwiches on brioche or other fine bread, with a thin mustard mayonnaise such as Durkee's sauce and your leftover jar of Bar-le-Duc (a luscious and famous currant jam from France) from dinner.

But since you have to roast the goose before you have goose left over, here is our procedure. For six to eight people, to have any leftovers, you will need a 12-pound goose.

There are many, many stuffings for goose, and one finds goose fanatics, like chili fiends or martini experts, who insist their stuffing is the *only* one. The goose itself is so greasy that the sausage stuffing we use for turkey or roast chicken would be inappropriate. As a personal idiosyncrasy which we do not ask you to share we do not care for the apple or prune stuffings many goose lovers demand. Nor do we go for the highly onioned, mashed potato stuffings, and a plain bread dressing is, to us, bland alongside such a rich meat.

For several years we followed a James Beard method—stuffing the goose with two or three pounds of garlic! As he promised, the meat was only delicately seasoned, not permeated with the garlic (which is discarded). The drawbacks are that the fat becomes too highly flavored for most uses, and the entire house smells for three or four days. So we settled for a discardable stuffing with less pungency.

Heat the oven to 325 degrees. In the wishbone or neck cavity, place an onion, halved; half a large apple or two halves of a small one; a rib of celery, cut or broken into two or three pieces. Skewer the neck skin to the back and put the wings akimbo behind the back.

Stuff the rear cavity similarly with apple, onion and celery. The proportions need not be exact; just use enough to hold the shape of the bird. Skewer or sew the cavity shut and truss the legs and wings. Salt and pepper the goose. Roast your 12-pound goose for five hours. Remove the fat from the bottom of the pan every 15 or 20 minutes; a bulb baster is good for this and prevents the burns you might get from spooning.

When done, let sit for 20 minutes, then untruss. The legs can be   103 removed and slices of meat cut from them, but we usually save the legs for cold leftovers. Do not slice the breast like a turkey, but instead cut long, quarter-inch strips of meat, each accompanied by a strip of the crisp skin.

The stuffing is discarded. If you insist on serving a stuffing-like dressing, you may place it either in an earthenware casserole or in an aluminum-foil package and cook it in the oven during the last hour the goose is cooking.

We'll not recommend a dressing recipe. They are easy to come by, and a whole book could be devoted to them.

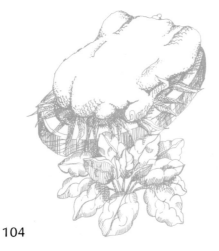

14

Happy New Year, Y'all

**Regional dishes,
with a southern sample menu**

WITH DEEP RESPECT to our Scandinavian friends in Minnesota, we just don't happen to like *lutfisk* or *lefse*. We do relish the *cioppino* and hangtown fry of San Francisco, the true crabcakes of Baltimore, the chili of West Texas and the clam chowder of either Boston or Manhattan. (We even like the unexpected Pacific Northwest version of clam chowder of which James Beard writes in *Delights and Pleasures*.) We use distinctive regional dishes much as we do non-French foreign dishes, either in coordinated regional menus or as accents in generalized meals. And once a year we go completely southern.

The southern tradition that eating blackeyed peas on New Year's Day brings luck throughout the year is only half tradition. Though the other half is a public relations gimmick, the custom is worth adoption by those not given to dyspepsia.

This pork-based menu features flavors sharp enough to cut through the numbed palate of a hard New Year's Eve, but tasty 105 enough to tempt the temperate. It departs from southern custom in that the salad follows the meat. Yet the salad is truly the climax of this meal, one we look forward to from one New Year's to the next.

Sazerac

Traditionally, your drinks will be based on bourbon or Maryland rye, either of which you can use in this New Orleans concoction. Because it is difficult to find Peychaud's bitters in some cities, you may, if you like, buy bottled, pre-mixed Sazerac and serve according to the label directions. This may, in fact, be more authentic than mixing your own, since the original recipe is still supposedly a secret. The following, however, comes close:

Using three sugar cubes for each two drinks, add two dashes of Peychaud's bitters and one dash of Angostura for each drink. Muddle with a wooden pestle, add ice and 2½ ounces of whiskey per drink, and stir.

In each chilled old fashioned glass, place one drop of Herbsaint, a Louisiana absinthe-substitute for which you, in turn, may substitute Pernod. Swirl it around and, if you are a purist and wasteful, pour it out.

Rub the rim of each glass with a nickel-sized piece of thin lemon peel, discard the peel, then place a fresh similar piece of peel in each glass. Strain the whiskey mixture into the glasses and serve without ice.

Shrimp Cocktail

Though it's better to use fresh green (raw) shrimp in the shell, the sleeping schedule of a New Year's morning usually dictates frozen, pre-cleaned shrimp. Follow the minimum cooking time of package directions, using as the cooking liquid a can or two of beer to which you've added the juice and shell of a lemon, salt, red pepper, parsley and bay leaves. Drain and chill well.

Rather than a tomato-based "shrimp dope," use this milder and
equally authentic Gulf Coast sauce: Combine 3 tablespoons chopped

shallots (scallions are not so good but can substitute) and two well-crumbled bay leaves with half a cup of mayonnaise and a third of a cup of cream. Age in refrigerator three hours before serving.

Fried Country Ham

You can buy packaged country (dry) ham slices, or you can follow our advice in the previous chapter for the small family's use of a whole ham. Trim off pepper coating and excess fat. Soak slices in warm water for 20 minutes. Rub a heavy skillet with ham fat or bacon. Starting with skillet cold, fry the slices over medium heat, turning frequently, until brown but not dry. Pour off most of the fat and set the skillet aside, *unwashed,* to use later in making the red-eye gravy which distinguishes the salad.

Vegetables

You will probably have to use frozen blackeyed peas and frozen mustard or turnip greens. Cook them with salt pork or a small, fat piece of ham to the upper limit of the cooking time shown on the package. (This is the only day of the year we overcook vegetables.)

Cornbread

Use your favorite recipe or a packaged mix; this is one bread for which a mix works fairly well. Cornbread may be enhanced, unless this menu is getting too porky for you, by scattering squares of half-cooked bacon over the top before baking.

Tennessee Hot Salad

We've encountered this salad under other names in various parts of Tennessee, Kentucky and Georgia, and we've read M.F.K. Fisher's description of a French family that always added a bit of pan gravy from roast beef or mutton to its Sunday salad.

On a large meat platter or in individual serving bowls, place a layer of bite-size leaf lettuce. Top this with layers of chopped radishes, chopped scallions including green tops, chopped dill pickles, chopped tomatoes from which the seeds and juice have been re- 107 moved, and slices of crisp bacon. (Slicing the vegetables and pickle makes the dish look prettier; chopping them makes it taste better.)

Just before serving, pour boiling-hot red-eye gravy over the salad. To make the gravy, add water and a little strong coffee to the skillet in which you fried the ham. Bring to a boil, stirring up the particles from the bottom of the skillet. Have additional cornbread ready to serve with the salad. Beer goes well with this meal. For dessert, serve Texas pecan pie (recipe on page 121) and coffee.

After this menu, pour additional coffee or beer and worship the football team of your choice.

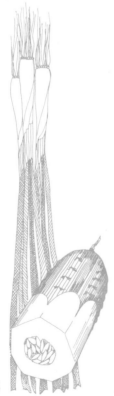

The Nonconvenience Foods

Soup and other ways to spend Sunday

THE MOST COMMON WATCHWORDS in food preparation today are "convenient" and "easy to prepare." These are not virtues to fault. Few cooks have not grabbed gratefully at a package of frozen vegetables or offered a prayer of thanks to whoever invented cornbread mix.

However, if you truly enjoy cooking as sport and hobby, much of the joy is in the doing. In this category, making soups and pasta from scratch rank high as pleasant ways to spend part of a weekend together.

Soups are simplest. Anyone who can dice vegetables and keep a kettle at "simmer" for a couple of hours can turn out excellent soup.

Begin with basics and learn to make a fine beef stock. Coerce your butcher into producing several rounds of beef shank and one or two bloody bones replete with marrow. The meat should fill about one quarter of your kettle space. Add an onion stuck with two whole cloves, a turnip and a carrot, both scraped and halved, several celery 109 ribs with leaves and a couple of parsley sprigs. Cover with cold water. Salt very lightly (reduction during cooking will concentrate the seasonings) and add four peppercorns.

Bring to a boil over medium heat, skimming away the foam with a slotted spoon. Reduce the temperature and simmer partially covered for an hour and a half; then uncover for an additional hour and a half to two hours cooking.

Correct the seasoning and strain through a colander. Set aside the meaty bones to cool. Dice meat and reserve. It either can be used in the vegetable soup that follows or substituted for roast beef in the "Absolute Hash" (page 101).

At this point, you have a choice between using all of your stock for one purpose or dividing it to make several soups. If you select the latter course, your best bet is to freeze the unused portion. If merely refrigerated, don't keep it over half a week. (We find used fruit juice jars make space-saving storage containers.) If all of your stock goes into one kind of soup, use a double boiler to reheat leftovers; that method cuts water loss.

Here are three ways to utilize the fruits of your afternoon's simmering.

Vegetable Soup

There are as many ways to make vegetable soup as there are cooks, and you'll learn to vary the content and seasoning of this version. Accompanied by a hefty green salad, a French or Italian loaf and a sharp cheese, this makes an excellent fall or winter lunch. In preparing, remember our advice on chopping time in "You Can't Go It Alone" and inveigle your partner into doing the salad.

Let us assume that you have three quarts of stock. Finely (and we mean finely) chop a large onion. Saute it in 1 tablespoon of butter until just transparent, not browned. Add stock and slowly bring to a boil. Have ready a quarter to half a cup of each of the following: cabbage, carrots, celery, green string beans, lima beans, potatoes and peas. Dice finely all but the limas and peas. Add some parsley. Whenever possible, use fresh vegetables or, if not available, frozen. Never add vegetables from a can; they'll make your homemade soup taste as though it came from one.

Once your broth is at a boil, add first the vegetables that cook longest; otherwise you'll end up with mush. Add first carrots and potatoes (20 minutes), then green string beans and limas (15 minutes) and finally the remainder of the vegetables (10 minutes). These are approximate cooking times for fresh vegetables; alter according to package directions if using frozen.

Simmer the soup just until the vegetables are tender. Add ⅓ teaspoon of thyme and, if you like, half that much sage. Correct seasoning. Add diced beef and heat through before serving.

Two simpler soups make just as good use of your stock. For the first version, cook rice in the boiling broth, varying the amount to suit the amount of stock. When the rice is tender (about 13 minutes), add the chopped soup meat reserved from making the original stock, heat through and serve with a dusting of Parmesan.

For the second version, cook wide, good-quality egg noodles, broken into small pieces, in the boiling stock. Simmer until the noodles are just tender. Add oregano to taste and boil briefly before serving.

You can achieve the same versatility with a rich chicken broth. Simply substitute chicken for the beef in the stock recipe. An interesting variation on the vegetable soup, using chicken stock, is to substitute rice for the starchier vegetables such as potatoes and lima beans. Season with a pinch of saffron.

Beef-Barley Soup

Recipes for navy bean and pea soups abound. Not so well known is what you can accomplish with barley and beef. This main course for lunch or supper serves eight. Make a full recipe even if you're fewer in number; refrigeration and reheating improves it.

Cover 1¼ to 1½ pounds of beef short ribs with 3 quarts of cold water. Add 1 cup pearled barley, 2 ribs celery (with leaves), 1 scraped carrot, 2 sprigs chopped parsley, a large onion stuck with 2 cloves, a large dried red pepper pod with seeds removed (or ¼ teaspoon red pepper flakes) and 1½ tablespoons salt.

Bring to boil over medium heat. Skim. Simmer uncovered for two hours. Remove celery, carrot, onion and pepper pod. Correct seasoning, adding black pepper if desired. Serve hot.

Milder barley soups, some suitable for the sickroom, are described on the barley box.

Duck Soup

When we discussed Szechuan duck (page 87), some parsimonious instinct led us to promise a way to use the rest of the duck. Some people don't like duck liver; we do. The following makes a snack for one or two.

In a 2-quart or 3-quart saucepan, place the reserved wings, giblets, neck and backbone (cut up or broken in two). Add a small onion stuck with 2 cloves, a rib of celery, salt, pepper and ¼ teaspoon ground thyme. Cover with water.

Bring to a boil and then simmer for at least an hour, removing and reserving the giblets as they become tender (liver first, then heart and gizzard). Add more water if needed. When flavor is hearty, skim off fat and strain the broth, discarding celery, onion, neck and backbone. Reserve the wings.

Add ¼ cup uncooked rice and ¼ cup chopped celery. Simmer until rice is done, about 13 minutes. Meanwhile, separate reserved wing meat, discarding skin and bones, and chop wing meat and giblets. Add them to the soup, correct seasonings, heat through and serve.

We've given you a flock of recipes that, if not meals in themselves, are at least hearty. Now we'll give you one that is a simple, elegant way to start off a multi-course dinner.

112

Clear Beef-Tomato Soup

You will need 3 cups of beef stock for this, which serves six. (We figure on half a cup per serving for first-course soups.) Halve 2 small onions and saute lightly in 2 tablespoons butter. Add broth, 6 medium tomatoes peeled and quartered, 1 clove garlic peeled but not cut, ½ teaspoon salt, a large rib of celery with leaves, a large bay leaf, ½ teaspoon dry basil and about eight grinds of the pepper mill.

Bring to a boil and simmer, partially covered, for an hour. Strain, adjust seasonings and serve very hot.

As arduous as making bread, making pasta at home is as pleasing to a basic creative urge. Noodles need no special equipment. Spaghetti requires a machine costing $25 or so and taking a storage space, depending on the brand of machine, about 10 inches long by 7 inches square. The same machine also makes noodles much easier. Ravioli *can* be made either without any special equipment or with a stamp (like a cookie cutter) costing less than $2. To do it right, however, you need a ravioli tray costing around $6.

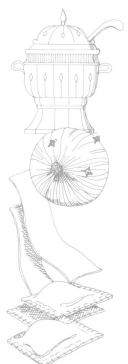

If you can buy hard flour such as semolina, your pasta will sharply improve. The kind of semolina sold for cereal purposes in a grind coarser than flour can be helped somewhat by 30 seconds at high speed in an electric blender. But lacking the hard flour, soft all-purpose flour still will make better pasta than even the finest commercial stuff.

We offer here an all-purpose recipe, but recommend again the book *Pasta* by Jack Denton Scott for more detailed and more specialized procedures.

Noodles

Heap 3 cups sifted flour on a bread board. Make a hollow in it and add 4 eggs. Blend with fingers. Keep kneading until the stiff, sticky, unmanageable mess starts to seem slightly manageable. Then knead some more.

113

When you finally have a dough that can be rolled to the thickness of—well, the thickness of a noodle—roll it out in a roughly rectangular shape. (It helps if you let the dough rest under a cloth for half an hour before rolling, but it's not absolutely essential.) Lightly brush the top surface of the dough with olive oil, then coil the dough like a jelly roll. Cut into desired widths, unroll and cook like packaged pasta, but not as long—about 2 minutes less or to your taste.

Why do we omit the usual instructions against overcooking? Because unless you already love pasta enough to want it cooked *al dente* (just to the bite), you'll not want to go to the trouble of making your own. In many cities, you now can buy fresh-made pasta, either already cut or in sheets of dough. The one brand of frozen fresh pasta we have tried, however, is a tasteless blah.

If you own a noodle machine, of course, the procedure outlined above becomes much simpler. Following the instructions that accompany the machine, you can eliminate about the last third of the hand-kneading by putting the dough through the machine several times at the thickest setting. Fold it back together each time until it comes out smooth. Then use a thinner setting each time until the sheet of dough is as thin as you want it. Ravioli trays come with instructions and a good enough recipe for the first try.

What sauces? If you're dedicated to tomato-based sauces (which we do not totally eschew), recipes are legion. But real appreciation of homemade pasta suggests one of these simple preparations:

• Drain the hot, cooked noodles and dump into a warm bowl with ½ cup of melted butter. Add ¼ cup of scalded cream, ½ cup of grated Parmesan, salt and pepper. Toss and serve at once.

• Sauce the drained, hot spaghetti with ½ cup hot olive oil in which finely minced garlic has been fried; toss with cheese, salt and pepper.

• With spaghetti, use only butter, cheese, salt and pepper.

• For a most unusual flavor, substitute grated Sap Sago cheese for the usual Parmesan.

   We urge you occasionally to use a mildly sauced, small serving of pasta as a first course, rather than as an accompaniment to meat.

   We also urge you get a professional manicure the day after making homemade pasta.

16

The Final Coup

**Desserts for people
who don't like dessert**

NOT EVERY ONE thrills to the mention of a Bavarian cream, the promise of a Spanish flan or the wonder of a baked Alaska—to say nothing of cookies and fruit cakes at Christmas time. Many an adult kicked the dessert habit and took the pledge on chocolate when we still thought it produced acne. Many others quit desserts when the bathroom scale shows them things they don't want to see. Others outgrow the habit and become as hard to please with desserts as youngsters are with vegetables.

But sometimes the meal or the occasion or both demand a course to follow the salad. Here are some desserts for people who don't, as a rule, like dessert.

The simple citrus desserts have obvious advantages. They are easy to prepare and low in calories compared with their pastry and cream relatives. They also can provide a light and sharp grace note to a heavy meal. Sliced oranges are favorites in the winter, when the

116

fruit is of fine quality and meals are heavy. A simple winter dinner might include a fine beef stew, pasta with butter and Parmesan, tossed green salad and slices of orange served with spices.

Spiced Oranges — Two Ways

The preparation is simple. Oranges should be at room temperature. Skin them, removing as much of the white fibrous material as possible, and slice in rounds ⅛ inch thick.

Then you have at least two choices: If the oranges are truly ripe, rub a light film of olive oil over the rounds with the tips of your fingers. Grind black pepper to taste over the surface. (This alternative makes a splendid appetizer, too.) Or, when sugar is needed, combine it with ground cloves and cinnamon (3 parts cinnamon to 1 part cloves) and sprinkle over the rounds. For both mixtures, allow the oranges to rest at least half an hour before serving.

Cheese in its infinite variety is a favorite dessert. Here are some special ways of presenting it that will tempt even the most hardened dessert hater.

Stuffed Guavas

Guava shells, available at specialty shops, are a particularly apt ending for a Mexican meal. Stuff them with cheese. A mixture of cream cheese and Roquefort, creamed at room temperature with a beater or wooden spoon, is ideal. Try 2 parts cream cheese to 1 part Roquefort, but alter proportion to your taste.

Cheese Torte

Humble cream cheese can make its contribution to an elegant and unusual torte as well. This version differs from the ordinary cheese cake enough to intrigue any guest.

Beat 4 egg whites until stiff and combine them with 1 cup sugar. Thoroughly cream 24 ounces of cream cheese and blend with the egg whites. Add one teaspoon vanilla. Pour into an eight-inch spring form 117 pan, three inches deep, that has been buttered and then dusted with ⅔ cup zwieback crumbs. Bake at 350 degrees for 25 minutes.

Then cover the top with a mixture of 2 cups sour cream, 2 tablespoons sugar and ½ teaspoon vanilla. Sprinkle with ⅓ cup toasted almond slivers. Bake 5 minutes longer at 475 degrees. Chill at least two hours.

Serve the torte with a slightly sweet sparkling wine, such as Asti Spumante or Lacryma Christi. Either will come as a pleasant surprise to guests who ordinarily abhor sweet sparkling wines.

Fruit and Gouda

Serve this cheese as finger food. Slice a baby Gouda in thin wedges and alternate with slices of ripe pear or apple in an overlapping arrangement.

Roquefort and Jelly

Serve a slice of Roquefort, a pat of butter and a spoonful of guava jelly on individual dessert plates. Have available either a crusty French or Italian loaf or a good grade of water biscuit. An excellent accompaniment is Cockburn's No. 85 Dry Club Port, one of the least expensive acceptable tawny ports.

Coeur à la Crème

A classic French dessert is Coeur à la Crème, heart-shaped individual desserts prepared in woven reed or ceramic molds. Recipes for the dish appear in many cookbooks, and no two seem to be alike. The ingredients combined with the cream may be cottage cheese, cream cheese or sour cream, with or without such additions as lemon juice, sugar or salt. This is the recipe we use:

Combine 8 ounces softened cream cheese, 8 ounces small-curd cottage cheese and 1 cup heavy cream. Mix, preferably with an electric mixer, until completely smooth. Line molds with cheesecloth, fill with the mixture, and fold cheesecloth over the top. Chill overnight, 118 with the molds resting on a plate to catch excess liquid.

This serves four to six, depending on the size of the mold. Usually the unmolded hearts are served with a sauce of strawberries. We prefer, however, to top them with a luxurious spoonful of Bar-le-Duc for each serving.

Poached Fruit

With little trouble, you can present an impressive dessert by poaching fruit either in water or wine. Pears, peaches and apricots are ideal candidates for this treatment. The fruit should be firm and not overripe, or it will turn into mush in the cooking process. Halve and pit or core the fruit, but peel only after cooking; the fruit skin imparts a lovely glow to the flesh as it cooks. Use enough water (or a half-and-half mixture of water and dry white wine) to cover the fruit halves. The amount of sugar will vary with the tartness of the fruit, but 1 cup sugar to 4 or 5 cups water is a good starting assumption. A teaspoon of lemon juice or an inch of vanilla bean may be added.

Bring syrup to a full boil before gently immersing fruit. Immediately reduce heat, cover and cook at a bare simmer. Cooking time will vary depending on ripeness and variety of fruit, but a gentle poke with a fork is a good idea after five minutes. The fruit is done when the fork enters easily without splitting. Overcooking produces an unappetizing mess. Peel the halves and chill before serving.

An appetizing variation for autumn and winter meals involves pre-poached pears. Scoop out their hollows. Fill with a mound of mincemeat and bake in a buttered dish at 350 degrees long enough to heat through, 5 to 10 minutes.

The marriage of fruits with liqueurs is an old dessert story. But a couple of versions deserve special mention. Both are ideal final courses for a hot summer day.

Melon in Spirits

This recipe requires a melon ball scoop and as many varieties of the fruit as you can find. Hollow out cantaloupe halves with the 119 scoop, reserving the shells. You might then combine the cantaloupe balls with balls of honeydew and watermelon, for example. Fill the shells with the melon mixture and add 1½ to 2 ounces of Myers rum or white crème de menthe. Serve with two short drinking straws for each serving and let your diners combine dessert with an after-dinner drink.

Strawberry Marnier

A simpler and at the same time more elegant dish is chilled strawberries with confectioner's sugar (the amount dependent on the tartness of the berries) and 1 tablespoon of Grand Marnier. To make a truly impressive appearance, serve the berries in stemware chilled to the frosting point. Top with a leaf or two of fresh mint, gently bruised to bring out the flavor.

The Chocolate Dessert

It isn't often that one comes across a dessert, or any dish for that matter, that is truly unique in its method of preparation. That description, however, fits a dish we refer to simply as "the chocolate dessert." The recipe was given us years ago by Professor and Mrs. William H. Warner, Jr., of the University of Minnesota. We believe it came from the kitchen of the senior Warners in Pittsburgh.

The dish is delicious and memorable. You'll enjoy the almost invariable reaction of guests who exclaim in praise and then in puzzlement, "But what is it? It's not a cake. It's not a pie. What is it?"

Here's what it is. And if the cooking method seems strange, please have the courage of our convictions and follow along.

7 ounces semi-sweet chocolate

7 ounces butter

7 ounces sugar (1 cup less 2 tablespoons)

7 eggs, separated

Melt butter over a low flame. Add chocolate and melt, taking care not to scorch. Remove from heat and add sugar. Cool, add egg yolks and beat 10 to 15 minutes with an electric beater. (If you do this by hand, it will take 30 to 45 minutes.) Fold in the stiffly beaten egg whites. Pour three-quarters of the batter into a well-greased spring form pan. Bake 35 minutes at 325 degrees. Let stand until cool. Pour the remaining raw batter on top. Sprinkle well with shaved semi-sweet chocolate and chill thoroughly. Cut into wedges for serving.

Texas Pecan Pie

We have a recipe for pecan pie, a heritage from a Texas childhood, that is essentially a praline in a pie crust. We've mentioned it twice as the perfect dessert for a spareribs cookout and a southern New Year's feast. Here's the recipe:

1 unbaked pie crust in 8½ inch pan

2 eggs

½ cup sugar

½ cup corn syrup (Light corn syrup is the north Texas style; some Georgia and east Texas recipes call for dark.)

2 tablespoons butter

¼ teaspoon vanilla extract

1½ cups pecan halves

Heat oven to 375 degrees. Beat the eggs lightly and mix in all other ingredients except the pecans. Fold in the pecans; they'll rise to the top during cooking. Pour into crust. Bake about 45 minutes until firm but still moist.

Although it is sweet, it's irresistible to all but the most determined dessert abstainers.

What to Cook When There's Nothing to Eat in the House

Omelets, rabbits of the Welsh persuasion and the versatile English muffin

WHEN WE don't feel like cooking, much less grocery shopping, our menu choices run like this:

1) Welsh rabbit and a celery salad

2) An omelet, either French or Spanish, filled with whatever appropriate leftover seems least obnoxious, and the simplest green salad for which materials are available

3) Mock pizza or another construction built around an English muffin

4) Sausages and potato pancakes.

Welsh rabbit. A dish, variously made, of melted or toasted cheese, often mixed with ale or beer, poured over toasted bread or crackers;—a jocose term, like "Cape Cod turkey" (codfish), that through failure to recognize the joke is commonly modified in cookbooks to **Welsh rarebit.**

123

Welsh rabbit: Add the beaten eggs, stirring, in a trickle at first, then faster as they begin to be absorbed.

The basic recipe is standard and simple. In the top of a double boiler (or in a heavy saucepan over an asbestos pad), melt a tablespoon of butter. Add ½ pound grated cheddar and these pre-measured dry ingredients: ½ teaspoon salt, ½ teaspoon dry mustard and a pinch of cayenne. Stir like crazy and, when the cheese begins to melt, add (in three or four splashes) half a cup of beer or ale seasoned with ½ teaspoon Worcestershire sauce.

When the beer seems absorbed, add (in a trickle at first, then faster as the mixture blends) two beaten eggs. Continue to cook, stirring, until the rabbit looks barely thick enough to serve (the second helping, which you'll want, will be thicker). Serve over crackers.

By varying the kind of cheese, from mild through the whitest and crumbliest Canadian, you adjust the flavor of the finished dish. By varying the beer, from a thin rice beer or American pilsner to a full-bodied stout or porter, you further change the dish. By using curry powder (maybe once a year if you make rabbit twenty times a year) instead of the mustard, you create something else again.

If the rabbit threatens to curdle even at low, low heat, or seems not to come together, drop your wooden spoon and switch to a whisk or rotary beater.

If you don't eat all of the rabbit while it's hot, the refrigerated leftover makes the best of cheese spreads. When hot, we offer paprika with the rabbit; when cold, black pepper from a mill.

Om'e·let, om'e·lette, *n*. (F. *omelette*.) Eggs beaten up with milk or water and cooked in a frying pan.

The omelet you know best is French, although the Spanish claim they invented that, too, as well as the other omelet called Spanish. Tomato sauce does not a Spanish omelet make; it's the frying method, and we can't remember when, if ever, we have served an omelet with tomato sauce.

The omelet is practically the only egg dish which you must cook quickly, not slowly. The pan must be heavy, round, spotlessly clean and well seasoned with cooking oil. (Heat oil in the pan, then cool and pour off the excess oil.) After fifteen years, we finally broke down and bought omelet pans which will never be washed, merely cleaned with paper towels and salt, and in which nothing but omelets ever will be cooked.

But we made an awful lot of successful omelets before we bought the specialized pans. It is best never to cook any acid ingredients in a pan which may be called on for an omelet. Unless food burns or sticks too tightly, clean the pan only with paper towels, salt and oil. If you must wash it, heat oil in the pan afterward, pour it off, dry the pan with a paper towel and wipe it again with oil.

Fortunately, even if you don't follow the practical advice above, you ordinarily can make very satisfactory omelets in just your own regular cast-iron kitchen skillet. You can wash it frequently (never in the dishwasher!) with water alone unless detergent or soap is absolutely required. After washing, dry with a paper towel and rub well with peanut oil.

The French Omelet

Allow two or three eggs per person, but don't try to use fewer than three or more than six to an 8-inch pan. Use a tablespoon of butter for three eggs and a teaspoon of water per egg. Beat the eggs and water until foamy with salt to taste and (if desired) white pepper or a drop of Tabasco. Heat the pan until almost smoking. Wear on your left hand a heavy oven mitt or barbecue mitt (unless the pan has a heat-proof handle or you're left-handed; in the latter case wear the mitt on your right). Add butter to the pan and swirl quickly to melt. Add the eggs.

With a fork, lift the first bits of egg that set so that more liquid can flow underneath to form layers. This takes practice. Too much stirring makes bad scrambled eggs. Too little makes a flat omelet. With your mitted hand, shake the pan back and forth to prevent sticking.

As the bottom becomes firm, tilt the pan and lift the edges of the 125

omelet with a small spatula to let more liquid from the top flow underneath. When omelet is brown on bottom and still moist on top, place filling (if desired) on the half of the omelet nearest the handle. Tilt the pan, handle side up, and gently roll the omelet over the filling. As the roll reaches the bottom of the pan, you can roll it right out on a serving plate. We'll discuss fillings later.

The Spanish Omelet

Eggs are the informing but not the principal ingredient of most Spanish omelets. The fillings make up most of the bulk. Here is an example of a typical Spanish omelet for two or four:

3 or 4 medium potatoes, peeled and sliced thin

1 large onion

½ cup olive oil

4 eggs

Salt and pepper to taste

Fry the potato slices lightly in the olive oil while chopping the onion. Push the potato slices aside, put onion on bottom of pan and cover it with the potatoes. Salt and pepper the mixture and cook until potatoes are done, chopping and mashing the mixture with a pancake turner until almost pureed and beginning to brown. Allow to cool at least 15 minutes—or several hours if you are preparing it ahead of time.

Put two eggs in each of two bowls and beat. Add half the potato mixture to each bowl and mix well. If the pan seems dry, add oil to barely cover the bottom. Heat until almost smoking. Add one bowl of the egg-potato mixture and spread over pan with spatula. No stirring. When bottom of omelet is brown, invert over it a plate just bigger than your omelet—and preferably just smaller than the outside rim of the pan. Wearing a mitt on each hand, grasp the pan and plate together and flip the whole thing over so that soft side of omelet falls onto the plate. Slip the omelet off the plate back into the pan, soft side down, and brown about three minutes.

127

French omelet: Tilt the pan, handle side up, as you gently roll the omelet down over the filling.

(Above) *Spanish omelet: Grasp the pan and plate together and flip the whole thing over so that the soft side of the omelet falls onto the plate.*
(Below) *Slip the omelet off the plate back into pan, soft side down.*

128

Remove the omelet, add more oil to pan if needed and cook the other half of the egg-potato mixture.

The filling? Generally speaking, fillings for Spanish omelets are cooked with the eggs; for French omelets they may either be mixed with the eggs or spread over the soft side before rolling.

Here are some fillings to be *mixed* with eggs in three-egg French omelets: ¼ cup of ham, bacon or salami, minced and crumbled; *fines herbes,* a quarter teaspoon or more each of parsley, basil, chervil and chives (a teaspoon each of any of the herbs you're lucky enough to have fresh); 2 teaspoons chopped and lightly sauteed onion.

Fillings to be *spread* over a French omelet before rolling could be: grated cheese, marmalade, a mild tomato sauce containing bits of lightly cooked chicken livers, chopped leftover vegetables in a cream sauce, or chipped beef in a cream sauce. For the last three, spoon more sauce over the rolled omelets.

For Spanish omelets, you may use chopped meats, potatoes, onions (or both, as above), beans, other leftover cooked vegetables, or you name it. You may also make four or so different kinds of Spanish omelets, stack them with a light sprinkle of paprika between layers and on top, then slice and serve in wedges like a cake.

After you've made omelets a few times, all this will become much simpler than it sounds.

English Muffins

Why do people so rarely think of using these ubiquitous leathery buns to make sandwiches? Lebanon bologna, lightly fried in butter, spread with Dusseldorf mustard and slapped between buttered, toasted English could put the hot dog out of business.

Cheese, melted on English under the broiler, with or without pizza sauce and flavorings, makes an open-faced treat. Or put half-cooked bacon over the cheese and broil open-faced. The variety of   129 things you can do keeps growing the more you think and match ideas to your taste.

Sausage and Potato Pancakes

There is absolutely no reason to believe that packaged, dehydrated potato pancake mix would turn out anything fit to eat, but if you try a few different brands, you'll find some which, surprisingly do. We try to keep some always on hand for days when we don't even have cheese or eggs. If you're lucky enough to have some leftover goose fat, it's great for frying them, but oil or shortening will do.

If you also have some Italian or Polish sausages, brown them in a little butter, then cover with ale and simmer until a fork easily pierces the skin (about 20 minutes). The combination of sausage and pancakes will tempt you to put off grocery shopping more often.

130

The Drinker's Dilemma

An eater's answer to the third-martini urge

DRINK IS the friend of gastronomy, but only up to a point. Good people inspire good talk, good talk inspires another drink and, by the time you get them to the table, even the most gracious of your good people may be slightly the worse for wear. So may we.

Though we'll not presume to pontificate about wines, we do serve good wines. The great French and German wines are so much in demand these days that the expense may usually keep them from our table, but not always. And even the merely good Spanish or Italian wines we use, or the increasing number of American wines which approach greatness, deserve a better consumer than the one who comes to the table after three or four martinis. (We also mix a better than average martini; it is our standard drink while we are working together on a meal for the two of us.)

We have made it a point most of the time when we entertain to *push* a particular pre-meal drink, to offer nothing else unless the guest insists, and to make our potion meet these criteria: 1) it is flavorful 131 enough not to seem insipid; 2) it is potent enough not to inspire boredom; 3) it is not potent enough to spoil the wines and foods that follow.

After dinner, we usually offer a wide variety of quite potent drinks, together with as much good *caffe espresso* as anyone wants. Thus, if anyone has a big head the next day, that's his business; at least he had an opportunity to enjoy dinner before developing the affliction.

So this chapter offers first a succession of premeal drinks. Our versions of the Bloody Mary, the Ratchet Screwdriver and Planter's Punch are best served before brunch or lunch. They actually make up a part of the meal and are too filling to serve before dinner. The others we suggest for afternoon or evening only.

Bloody Mary

In each chilled 6-ounce bubble glass, sprinkle enough celery salt to lightly cover the bottom. Add the juice of ¼ lime and a scant ½ teaspoon of Worcestershire sauce. Then add 1½ ounces freezer-chilled, 80 proof vodka (100 proof only if you insist) and half of an 8-ounce can of chili-pepper flavored tomato juice. (If only ordinary tomato juice is available, or you prefer, add cayenne or Tabasco to taste.) Crush a pinch of basil between the fingers and add. Stir, add ice cubes to fill the glass and garnish with a 5-inch piece cut from the leafy end of a celery rib.

The Ratchet Screwdriver

The mixture of even freezer-chilled vodka with even freshly squeezed orange juice tends to taste diluted as the watered alcohol (that's the vodka) cuts the orange flavor. Fill out the flavor (and change the color) with a dash or more of Grenadine.

Planter's Punch

In a blender (a cocktail shaker will do, but it takes a big one and a lot of shaking), place for each drink the following: 1 tablespoon lime juice, 2 crushed ice cubes, 2 shots (3 to 4 ounces) of punch rum (we use Myers) and 1 tablespoon brown sugar (we prefer dark). Blend until frothy.

Serve over additional crushed ice in a tall glass with straws. Garnish with a maraschino cherry, or an orange or lime slice, or all of these, if you like.

The Tall Negroni

Though it is not original with us, we've been unable to remember just where we first found the idea of embellishing a Negroni with a little more gin and some soda water. We've had it made by bartenders from Los Angeles to Montreal, but we always had to give them step-by-step directions—except in New York and Philadelphia, where you simply say, "Make a Negroni with an extra half-shot of gin, put it in a tall glass and add soda."

In any event, this drink, described in the first chapter of this book (page 16), is our all-time favorite pre-dinner solution to the drinker's dilemma. Its regular appearance at our home also has led to the increasing presence of Bitter Campari behind Washington bars; *our* friends serve the drink to *their* friends, who then ask their bartenders to stock the ingredients.

Because it is slightly sweet and yet still successful, the Negroni is a good introduction to the next three drinks. We have learned that an unexpected but not unpleasant sweetness makes the habitual dry-drink guest slow his sipping enough to enjoy the meal.

Kir

This is a favorite lunch drink at Chez Camille, Washington. We don't know how Camille makes it, but at home we make it thus: In an 8-ounce goblet or wine glass, place two ice cubes, 1 tablespoon of crème de cassis and a twist of lemon peel. Fill with dry white wine and stir.

Vermouth Cassis

Use the package recipe on the bottle of crème de cassis. Then try it again using just a little less crème de cassis. Add about 8 parts vermouth to 1 of cassis; adjust soda to your taste.

Sazerac

For a nonauthentic but successful version (and one which may make scotch drinkers discover a few merits in bourbon or Maryland-style rye), see page 106.

Neither of us has ever had a successful Tom and Jerry, no matter how happy the recipes may sound. The only memorable eggnog either of us has had is our holiday favorite, "Blanche Knopf's Eggnog," from Craig Claiborne's *An Herb and Spice Cookbook.* Therefore we offer, as below-zero drinks:

Cappuccino Presto

There once was a neighborhood quarrel in which each family demanded the other speak first. Neither would, until a large (for Washington) snowfall in which each family found itself shoveling not only its own walk but also half (per family) of the elderly neighbors' walk between us. We invited the enemy in for a warm-up drink, have been friends ever since, and recommend this fast mixture for winter warm-ups, with or without quarrels. In each 8-ounce mug, place:

    1 tablespoon (scant) of instant espresso coffee

    1 tablespoon (scant) of powdered chocolate drink mix

    1 ounce of good brandy

For each drink, heat one cinnamon stick with 6 ounces skim milk (or homogenized milk mixed with water; remember that in the mixture of cocoa and coffee you're preparing, the cocoa would have been made with milk and the coffee with water). Lift the cinnamon stick into a mug with tongs and then pour the milk mixture in, stir and serve. Get warm quickly.

Hot Buttered Rum

This cliché drink is best if mixed small and potent. For each drink, muddle in a 6-ounce ceramic cup or mug 2 teaspoons of dark brown sugar with a dash of Angostura bitters and a large (2-ounce) shot of dark Jamaica rum. Heat ½ cup water with a cinnamon stick, 2 whole cloves, a whole allspice and a cardamom seed crushed between the fingers. When water boils determinedly, lift cinnamon sticks into each cup or mug with tongs and strain the remaining liquid into the cups. Stir at the last minute and float a pat of butter on each cup.

Saint George

We don't believe this drink yet, but its recipe was sold to us a few years ago when one of us was editor of *Potomac,* the Sunday magazine supplement of *The Washington Post.* It was test-tasted in the company of Donald Dresden, restaurant critic of that newspaper, with the immediate bartender being Camille Richaudeau, proprietor of Washington's Chez Camille. It works.

When you are terribly fatigued or discouraged, mix in a wine glass:

½ teaspoon freshly squeezed lemon juice

½ teaspoon Grenadine

2 ounces well chilled Amer Picon

2 ounces well chilled strong ale or beer (we recommend Bass or Ballantine Ale)

Drink the unlikely thing and feel better. Do not drink a second: it will taste as bad as you expect the first to taste. But so long as you forego the second, the first one is . . . *superbe!*

After-dinner drinks should include a good Cognac (none of the 3-star Cognacs you settle for in restaurants qualify), or alternatively a good Armagnac, more suitable to American tastes and less expensive; a scotch and at least one other kind of whiskey, and a few liqueur-

135

type things. Be sure also to include a large and unlimited quantity of dark-roast coffee, preferably *espresso*.

It is not so much for company as for two cooks alone that we suggest a few almost forgotten post-meal drinks.

Alexander the Great

This drink was originally and properly called simply an Alexander. In recent years, the substitution of good brandy for gin has turned it into a breakfast drink or a hangover cure. With the juniper bite of the gin restored, it deserves belated attention. Try it. For each drink, combine in a blender:

1 ounce creme de cacao

2 ounces good, strong gin (94 proof or better)

1 tablespoon heavy cream

2 small ice cubes or 1 large one, crushed

Blend the hell out of it and serve, uniced but cold, in a cocktail glass. Garnish with a hazel nut.

The Easiest Pousse-Café

In a liqueur glass, carefully pour over a spoon (so that the liquids go smoothly down the side of the glass instead of splashing in the middle) a teaspoon or so of each of the following:

Brandy

Creme de cacao or Kahlua

Heavy cream

"Cold Medicine"

The ultimate cold cure has nothing to do with cuisine or the table; it is often, however, a late-night production of two in the kitchen. For each 8-ounce mug, place in a saucepan 6 ounces of water, a cinnamon stick, 2 whole cloves, an allspice and the hull of half a lemon (whose juice has already gone into the mug). Bring to a boil. While waiting, place in the mug the juice of another half lemon, 2 teaspoons sugar (white or brown), and 1½ to 2 ounces of spirits— 136 rum, gin, bourbon, brandy, or Maryland or Canadian rye. Place the cinnamon stick in the mug with tongs, then strain the boiling water into the mug. Drink and get well quickly, though no efficacy claims are made under the Food, Drug and Cosmetic Act as amended.

137

When entertaining, you can set the table hours ahead of time or even the day before.

More Easy Elegances

Some menus to end it all

AN EARLIER CHAPTER, "You Can't Go It Alone," started with the challenge, "So you like to cook."

That's not enough. You may be capable of producing splendid soup, vegetables that aren't mush, a distinguished roast, and a dessert that really convinces the sweets-haters that they've been missing something. But unless the two of you can put them together in ways that satisfy you and your family or guests, it all comes to naught.

In earlier chapters, we've suggested menus without explaining the basic rationale behind the planning—except where we've written about meals that require two cooks because of time-consuming or complex preparation.

Menu planning demands a degree of transference, an ability to conjure up images of what the food will look like, how it will taste and how the diner will feel afterward. If you're new to this pleasant game (much more fun played doubles than singles), it will require 139 some conscious effort. But if you like to cook and like to eat, these judgments will soon become semi-automatic. (It may surprise you how often you and your partner have the same kitchen idea at the same instant.) You will immediately reject the idea of serving sole, potatoes and cauliflower on the same plate without having to reason that all-white belongs in weddings rather than on dinner plates.

As a way to escalate to automatic, here are some factors to think about on a conscious level at first:

Taste—Subjected to a pre-wedding spree of experimental cooking, the gentle father of one of us tactfully suggested that it might not be a good idea to have every dish in a meal highly seasoned. That gentleman had been served a fenneled and garlicked pork chop that would have made our ancestors (Italian) proud. Other ancestors (German) would have reveled in the sauerkraut with juniper berries and white wine, and still others (French) the tarragon salad dressing. The total man (second generation) had a bellyache of international origin.

We have discovered that the best way to prevent unpleasant aftereffects is to plan a simple meal around one or two dishes. Don't make a production of every dish. Let us say, for example, that you are preparing a fillet of fish with a rich cheese sauce or with a spicy, tomato-based topping. The remainder of the meal falls into place—a boiled new potato; peas or green beans, the latter perhaps with a touch of oregano, the former with mint; salad with a simple oil and vinegar dressing.

Texture—No slippery noodles and slick okra on the same plate, please. You can also eliminate meals starting with cream soups, middling with scalloped potatoes and arriving at a milky custard finale.

Color—Planning the winter dinner described later in this chapter, we thought sliced celery braised in bouillon would be a satisfactory complement to Cornish hen. The mild flavor wouldn't fight with the bird; the crisp texture would provide a pleasant contrast. Looking at it with the eyes of a photographer, one sees a pale tan main dish and a light green accompaniment. Forget it.

Appetite—The clean plate club went out with World War II, and so did the theory that one must consume incredible amounts of food to remain nutritionally viable. A hearty soup, salad, fruit and cheese make a delightful lunch. A protein course, vegetables (starchy and non), salad and dessert make an acceptable dinner. For more elaborate meals, cut the size of servings sharply. Pasta makes a fine first course—but in a small mound, please, not as cover for a dinner plate.

Here are four menus that attempt to avoid the pitfalls we've described. One is for winter, two are for summer, and one is a meal for all seasons. Our winter offering reads like this:

Boula-Boula
Shrimp or Crab Legs
Cornish Hen With Wild Rice
Baked Mixed Vegetables
Endive and Mushroom Salad
Orange Custard

Boula-Boula

Combine canned turtle consomme with canned, noncondensed pea soup in equal parts. Mix thoroughly. Heat to boiling and serve, accompanied to table by a bowl of salted (and thus unsugared) whipped cream to which the diner helps himself.

Serve the seafood with the cream mayonnaise described on page 106; cook your own shrimp or buy cooked crab legs.

Cornish Hen with Wild Rice

Stuff the Cornish hen with wild rice (see page 95), with butter and ½ teaspoon of thyme per bird added. Truss and roast according to the bird's wrapper directions.

Baked Mixed Vegetables

Prepare a baked vegetable casserole like the one presented by Myra Waldo in *The Round-the-World Cook Book*. The recipe serves six. Peel and slice thin half a dozen medium sized baking potatoes and spread them in a shallow buttered pan. Combine 4 tomatoes, peeled and chopped; 3 carrots, sliced thin; 2 onions, chopped fine; 2 cloves of garlic, minced, and 3 tablespoons chopped parsley. Season with 1½ teaspoons salt and ½ teaspoon pepper. Spread the vegetable mixture over the potatoes and add 2 cups of water. Bake in a 375-degree oven for 45 minutes. Pour ¼ cup of olive oil over the vegetables and bake for an additional 15 minutes.

A rich white California wine such as Pinot Chardonnay would be an excellent accompaniment to the main course.

Endive and Mushroom Salad

To prepare the salad, dress the endive (cut either in rings or in quarters lengthwise) and the mushrooms (small, fresh and raw) with a lemon juice and olive oil combination using the same proportions as you would to make a vinegar and oil dressing—1 part acid to 3 or 4 parts oil.

Orange Custard

Dessert is orange custard, a flavorful concoction that includes a high ratio of egg whites to yolks. We've adapted to our own taste Barbara Norman's recipe from *The Spanish Cookbook*. It serves six.

3 cups milk

1 cup sugar

3 egg yolks

9 egg whites, beaten until stiff

grated peel of 2 medium oranges and 1 small orange

Combine in blender or with mixer the milk, sugar, grated peel of 2 oranges and egg yolks. Pour into bowl and fold in beaten egg whites thoroughly. Strain mixture into the upper part of a large double boiler, adding the grated peel of the small orange. The water in the

142

bottom of double boiler should be hot but not boiling. Stir occasionally with a whisk, keeping an eye out for lumps. If lumps do form and can't be taken care of with the whisk, use a mixer. Cooking time usually runs between 20 and 30 minutes; the final product should have the consistency of a heavy cream sauce. Pour the custard into individual dessert dishes and chill.

Here's a menu for summer:

Gazpacho

Veal Scallops

Sauteed Zucchini

Dill Salad

Lime Ice Cream

The best recipe we know for gazpacho, that splendid Spanish cold soup, calls for a small amount of tomato paste in the basic mixture. Unlike some other recipes, it happily calls for a small spread of mixed chopped vegetables as a garnish for the finished soup.

Gazpacho

(This recipe serves 12. Even though your diners may be fewer, the soup freezes well. After thawing, however, it must be reconstituted with a run through the blender or a thorough workout with the whisk, since the oil will become separated.)

2 medium onions, coarsely chopped

2 medium bell peppers, split, seeded and coarsely chopped

10 medium tomatoes, peeled, seeded and coarsely chopped

4 medium cucumbers, peeled and coarsely chopped

1⅓ tablespoons garlic, finely chopped

8 cups bread, torn into chunks, with no crusts allowed. French bread is good; a good brand of standard white will suffice if it is several days old

8 cups cold water

½ cup red wine vinegar, the less acidulous the better

2⅔ tablespoons salt

½ cup olive oil

2 tablespoons tomato paste

Stir together onions, peppers, tomatoes, cucumbers, garlic and bread. Combine water, vinegar and salt; add to the vegetable mixture. Fill the jar of an electric blender a third full with part of this mixture; blend at medium speed for a few seconds, then at high speed until the mixture is smooth. Pour into a large bowl; then fill the blender jar a third full again, blend as above, and repeat a third of a jar at a time until all is pureed in the blender and poured into the bowl. Combine olive oil and tomato paste; beat into the puree with a whisk.

Refrigerate the soup in a covered bowl until thoroughly chilled. Before serving, whisk the soup to recombine any oil which may have separated. Add a dash of Tabasco, if you like. Garnish with a finely chopped mixture of cucumbers, onion and peppers. For a pleasant crunch, add a few croutons that have been browned and crisped in olive oil over medium heat, then drained on paper toweling.

Veal Scallops

The scallops of veal should be pounded thin. Rub with garlic and season with salt and pepper on both sides. Dip briefly into beaten egg, then press each side into bread crumbs, made in the blender or by hand. Refrigerate half an hour. Saute each side in a half-and-half mixture of butter and olive oil until golden brown, 3 to 4 minutes.

Sauteed Zucchini

Scrape the zucchini with a plastic scrubber under running water. Slice in ⅛-inch rounds. Since the veal and zucchini require two frying pans, they may require both cooks, one for each. Saute the zucchini lightly in olive oil at moderate heat, turning once. The cooking will take remarkably little time, perhaps 3 minutes. Sprinkle with salt, pepper and Parmesan. Accompany the meat and vegetable course with a good white wine such as an Italian Soave.

Dill Salad

Salad with dill dressing is best prepared with Boston or bibb lettuce, watercress and fresh dill. If you are fortunate enough to have dill from your garden or even from a produce stand, snip off about a tablespoon and a half of it to serve salad for four. Cut finely. Rub the dill in small quantities between the palms of your hands before sprinkling over the cleaned greens. Dress with 3 parts oil and 1 part vinegar. If you must content yourself with dried dill, start with half a teaspoon, toss the salad, and add more as you like.

Lime Ice Cream

This rich recipe came from a manufacturer of ice cream freezers, but could be frozen in a refrigerator freezing compartment as well. To produce 1½ quarts, combine the following:

4 eggs
1 cup sugar
½ cup corn syrup
3 cups milk
1 cup lime juice (preferably freshly squeezed)
1 tablespoon grated lime rind
1 cup heavy cream

Freeze in a hand-powered or electric-powered freezer according to manufacturer's directions. Or place in ice trays, freeze until mushy, remove and beat with an electric beater until smooth; repeat the process. Then pack into plastic freezer containers, cover and freeze until hard.

"Simple" Summer Cold Plate

Our second summer menu suits a scorching day when, although you are unwilling to expend either time or energy, you are willing to put forth some money.

For this one-plate meal, line the plates with bibb lettuce. Mound on each plate half an ounce of the best caviar you can afford. Accompany with good water biscuits. Select a ripe cantaloupe or honeydew melon. Cut in eighths and remove the rind with a grape- 145 fruit knife. Wrap each slice with paper-thin prosciutto ham and secure with a toothpick.

Then prepare Steak Tartare. When this dish is the mainstay of the meal, we prefer to serve the unmixed meat and egg yolk with a tray of condiments and let each diner mix his own. For this menu, however, it works best to mix all in the kitchen. Start with the freshest ground top sirloin or round steak you can find. (If you have a meat grinder, grind your own.) For each half pound of meat (which serves two), add the yolks of 2 eggs, 1 teaspoon of capers, 1 tablespoon of chopped onion (or to taste), 1 teaspoon Worcestershire, 1 tablespoon chopped parsley, a dab of Dijon or similar prepared mustard, a dash of Tabasco and 1 teaspoon of Cognac or Armagnac. Mix lightly and add salt if desired. (For this menu, we omit the anchovies which ordinarily are part of Steak Tartare.) Offer paprika at table, and serve the meat with an ice cream scoop.

The last elements for our "simple summer cold plate" are a tin of truffled paté and a good champagne, French or domestic. There's no need for dessert.

Finally, here is a collection of courses that will please you and your guests in any season.

Consomme Julienne
Steak Diane
Wild Rice with Mushrooms and Bacon
Salad with Brie
The Chocolate Dessert

Consomme Julienne

Undertake a labor of love and make your own double consomme. Prepare the beef stock described earlier (page 109). After straining it through a colander, strain again through a double layer of cheesecloth. Cool to room temperature. Add 2 whipped egg whites (frothy but far from stiff) and 2 crushed egg shells for every quart of bouillon. Boil all together for 3 minutes. Strain once more through a double layer of cheesecloth or an old linen towel. (We say *old* because that towel will never be the same again.)

Garnish the consomme with finely cut slivers of turnip, celery and carrot, all cooked in salted water until just tender. Bring the soup just to the boil immediately before serving.

Steak Diane

You probably won't be able to prepare Steak Diane for more than four; indeed, it is an ideal dish for two. Although Steak Diane costs $10 or more when served at a restaurant (just because it is cooked at table), it is one of the simplest ways to prepare steak.

Some chefs add Worcestershire, Dijon mustard or even Tabasco to Steak Diane. We prefer not. Be extravagant and accompany this course with a good Burgundy.

For each person, pound a small Delmonico or New York strip steak with the flat of a *choy doh* or with a meat mallet until steak is very thin. Pre-measure and take to table for each two servings:

a lump of sweet butter (about 1 tablespoon)

a slightly larger lump of sweet butter in which a teaspoon or more of chives have been creamed

4 ounces sherry

2 ounces Cognac or Armagnac

Melt the plain butter in a chafing dish and brown a steak on both sides. Roll it up with tongs or long fork and shove to one side of pan. Brown the other steak or steaks.

Heat the brandy in a ladle; ignite it with chafing dish flame, and pour over the steaks. When the flame expires, add the chive butter and sherry and bring to a simmer. Serve the steaks, and pour the sauce over both the steaks and wild rice.

Wild Rice with Mushrooms and Bacon

Follow the procedure for cooking wild rice given on page 95. Toss the rice with fresh, small mushroom caps sauteed in just enough 147 butter to lightly coat the grains of rice. Sprinkle with crisp bacon bits.

Go back to our first chapter, page 21, and repeat the tomato salad with Cognac. Serve it with ripe Brie, water biscuits or good French bread, and the remains of the Burgundy.

The final course for this meal is that strangely concocted chocolate dish from page 120.

As you progress both as cook and as observant diner, you will become the author of your own culinary elegances—and practicalities, too.

Epilogue

On grocery shopping

SENATOR HART and Justice Douglas have been seen at our neighborhood supermarket, but the best-known and most celebrated shopper there is Begonia Berrybuster. She won the Golden Baskart as Supermarket Shopper of the Year three times, retiring the trophy before her own semiretirement from active competition. She gave us a sample of the instruction she offers selected pupils in an effort to perpetuate her art.

Tripping a cripple in order to seize the first baskart in a line of 23, Begonia looked like everybody's grandmother as she parallel-parked in front of the ground meats and started to shop for short ribs.

"Always put your cart someplace you don't want to buy anything," she explained, "but keep a hand on it at arm's length. That way you can cut off other customers from three or four items at a time."

As she pulled away from the next counter, a young man politely withdrew his own shopping cart to let her pass. She immediately pulled ahead of him and wedged his cart against the mayonnaise.

"Never let a courtesy go rewarded in the grocery store," she lectured. "The strife you waive may be foregone."

The young man gently pushed at her cart, attempting to make his own way through a narrow space past ketchup into jelly.

"Officer, officer!" shouted Begonia to the store security guard, "this oaf is molesting me!"

As the company cop hurried over and the young man turned in alarm, Begonia deftly kicked his cart three departments back into dog food and plunged her own cart into the maelstrom of dairy.

149

"Here is the real test of a champion," she confided. "The dairy department is always a busy one, because you find side aisles and main aisles crossing."

She stopped her cart in an intersection, turning it out into the dairy aisle, and carefully examined six half-gallon cartons of milk before buying a pint of yogurt. Traffic was stopped three ways.

"That was just for practice," she chuckled. "Wait until we get to canned soups. Then I can cut off juices, salad oils and gourmet foods with just one *grand jeté* and a countermarch of the baskart."

Though her sumo wrestler's build makes her expert at the solo game, she admires and teaches the subdisciplines of multifooted supermarket technique.

"If you see a friend in the store, time your shopping to meet her in produce. That way you can block mushrooms and spinach, she can block squash and corn, and your carts can tie up tomatoes and garlic for thirty or forty people during a ten-minute conversation."

Mrs. Berrybuster is not insensitive to the skills of supermarket employes themselves.

"Their stock carts are bigger than our baskarts, and they always choose the busiest moments to stock the busiest areas."

She sees great hope for American youth.

"Nobody can block a supermarket aisle as well as a pair of uncontrolled kids," she said. "And if they have a mother who knows our motto, 'Think thoughtless!' not even a champion like me can outshop them."

She moved to the customer service counter to get her check approved, but carefully waited until she was at the head of a line of five persons before writing it.

"The kind of aggressiveness required for successful supermarket shopping offers the real hope for America today," said Begonia, fervor burning in her eyes. "The bleeding hearts and etiquette-hounds have emasculated our society, and it's up to us to put the teeth back into it!"

150

Appendix

WE WARNED YOU to buy a spice rack three times larger than you think you need. In it you'll keep things like vanilla extract and cream of tartar as well as true herbs and spices. The lists here omit things like soy sauce and special oils which you'll keep with the vinegars, etc., as well as such things as Chinese plum sauce which belong in the refrigerator. But here's what will make your spice rack overflow:

Essential

Peppercorns, black and white
  and a mill to grind them
Cinnamon, sticks and powdered
Thyme
Bay leaf
Basil
Dry mustard
Tarragon
Rosemary

Ginger, powdered
  but it's well to have fresh ginger in
  the refrigerator
Oregano
MSG
  monosodium glutamate, sold either
  as MSG or under various trade names,
  such as Accent

Frequently Used

Allspice, whole and powdered
Anise (or substitute fennel)
Cayenne
Celery salt
  chiefly for Bloody Marys
Chervil
Chili powder
  check the flavor of the brand you
  buy; you may want to correct it by
  adding hot pepper, cumin, or
  oregano, or any two of these
Clove, whole and powdered
Dill
  the fresh is incomparably better, but
  dried is useful
Marjoram

Nutmeg, whole
  and get a grater to grate your own
Paprika
  the sweet Hungarian, not the hot
  Spanish
Pepper flakes (red)
Saffron
  the world's most expensive seasoning,
  used in such small quantities that
  your budget can stand it
Turmeric
  or substitute a smaller quantity of
  dry mustard
Five spices powder (Chinese)
Szechuan peppercorns

151

Occasionally Used

Caraway

Cardamom
powdered most frequently used, but whole seeds are delicious in coffee or fruit drinks

Celery seed

Chives
better fresh or frozen, but dried ones help in emergencies; a stronger, but acceptable flavor, is obtained by substituting finely chopped fresh scallion greens, perhaps in smaller quantity

Coriander, seeds or powder
have uses of their own, but in dishes where the fresh leaves are needed, are a poor substitute

Cumin

Curry powder
but don't be upset if a curry recipe doesn't call for it; curry powder is a blend of spices, and some recipes— the best ones—call not for pre-mixed curry powder but for the individual component spices such as cardamom, cinnamon, coriander, mustard, pepper, etc.

Fennel seeds
or substitute anise

Juniper berries

Mace
or substitute nutmeg, of which mace is the outer coating

Mint
best fresh, but dried is occasionally useful in winter

Mustard seeds, white and black

Poppy seeds

Sage

Savory

Sesame seeds

Horseradish powder
but horseradish is better freshly grated, or even out of a bottle, with the liquid squeezed out of the bottled variety

Star anise (Chinese)

Rarely Used

Gumbo filé
Spice parisienne
Composed salts

Obviously the above lists are a matter of personal taste. We'll not quarrel with anyone who disagrees with a classification or with the omission of an herb or spice.

The green herbs listed, such as oregano, basil, tarragon, are much more pungent in their fresh form and thus preferable if you can find or grow them. But use three or four times more of the fresh herb than the dried.

Recipe Index

153

Index by Nationality

Where a recipe is derived from a given cuisine but not authentically a part of it, and in cases where a dish has crossed borders into other cuisines, a second nationality is indicated in *italics*.

Out of peppercorns —

Clean watercress

½ gal. Scotch
½ gal. Bourbon
½ gal. gin
        vodka
        rum
        tomato juice

Szechuan duck

    Supermarket:

Duck
Scallions
Fresh ginger
peanut oil
Chinatown:

        tonic
        soda
        ginger
    how I hate
        cocktail

hamburger
cheese for school lunches
yoghurt   "   "   "
lunch meat "   "   "
dishwasher detergent
toilet tissue
salad greens
we're low on salt
ENGLISH
salt

...who cooks a scrambled egg
...sponsible for cleaning (and
...ing) the skillet.
...se do not put carbon steel
...in the dishwasher; they
...washed by hand, honed
        and OILED.

Joe —

    We've
wine got only
glasses   seven

    Je t'aime

Whatever happe
t Beverly Le
Chinese cookbook
need it